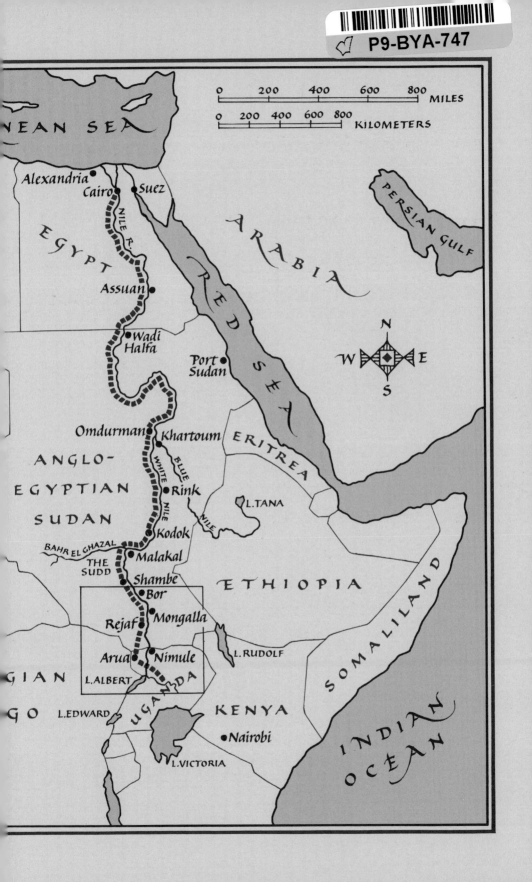

David & Florence —
with deep
appreciation
and
warm friendship.

Dr. & Ron

Vermont Weekend
February '93

CHRONICLES OF A SECOND AFRICAN TRIP

George Eastman and His Traveling Companions.
Eastman is at center; from left to right in front are
Dr. Albert Kaiser, Osa Johnson, Martin Johnson (behind Osa), and,
in the ten-gallon hat, the professional hunter, Phil Percival.
Behind them are the unidentified Africans, probably personal gunbearers.
(*Martin Johnson photo.*)

CHRONICLES

OF A

SECOND

AFRICAN TRIP

by GEORGE EASTMAN

Edited and with Notes and an Introduction
by Kenneth M. Cameron

The Friends of
the University of Rochester Libraries
ROCHESTER · NEW YORK
1987

KENNETH M. CAMERON, *author of fourteen novels
and two Off-Broadway plays, and co-author of four theater
texts, has taught at several major institutions including
the University of Rochester. He has received writing awards
from the Ford Foundation, the American Place Theater,
and RCA-NBC. An enthusiastic East African traveler,
he made his most recent trip in a four-wheel-drive truck
accompanied by a cook and a driver.*

ELIAS MANDALA, *a member of the Department of History
of the University of Rochester, is a specialist
in African economic history with a particular interest in
the history of agricultural change on that continent.
Professor Mandala is a native of Malawi.*

ACKNOWLEDGEMENTS

THIS *book would have been impossible without the help of many people. I am particularly indebted to Margaret S. Butterfield for permission to use her husband's notes; to Mary Huth and Carl Kabelac of the University of Rochester Libraries; to Robert Mayer, David Wooters, Michael Hager, Carolee Aber, Jeff Baker, and Luis Alberto Martinez of the International Museum of Photography at George Eastman House; to Sondra Updike Alden and Barbara Henshall of the Martin and Osa Johnson Safari Museum; and above all to Catherine D. Hayes, until recently Associate Director of the University of Rochester Libraries, and Horace Hart and Mrs. James S. Gleason of the Friends of the University of Rochester Libraries.*

KMC

[*vii*]

CONTENTS

Foreword   xiii

Introduction   xvii

CHRONICLES OF A SECOND AFRICAN TRIP   3

Notes   79

Bibliography   89

ILLUSTRATIONS

Photographs have been selected to fit the manuscript and to illustrate, as much as possible, George Eastman's interests. As a result, a wealth of ethnographic photographs by Martin Johnson have not been included. Both men are credited here with photographs in which they also appear: apparently, they set up the shots and had someone else release the shutter.

		facing page
Frontispiece: George Eastman and His Traveling Companions.		v
1. Setting Sail.		3
2. Egyptian-Sudanese Train.		8
3 and 4. Crew Members of the *Dal.*		10
5. At the Khartoum Zoo.		12
6. Eastman's Floor Plan of the *Dal.*		15
7. The *Dal.*		16
8. Osa and Dr. Kaiser on the *Dal.*		18
9. A Stop on the Nile.		20
10. A Dinka Village on the Nile.		23
11. The Kodak King at Kodok With His Kodak.		24
12. In the Sudd.		27
13. Wheelhouse of the *Dal.*		28
14. Eastman With Crocodile.		31
15. Hunting on the Nile Shores.		32
16. Eastman's Gunbearer.		34
17. Motor Safari.		37
18. Medical Examination.		38
19. Avanti!		40
20. Rest Camp.		45
21. Eastman Pasha.		47
22. The White Rhino.		48

23. The White Rhino at the Taxidermist's.   50

24. A Screened Dining Room.   53

25 and 26. Foot Safari.   56

27. Waiting for Elephant.   58

28. Elephant.   61

29. The Tusk.   62

30. The Elephant at the Taxidermist's.   64

31. At Eastman House.   67

32. Martin and Osa Johnson.   68

33 and 34. Kaiser's Elephant Hunt.   73

35. Nile Perch.   74

36. Down the Nile.   76

Martin Johnson photos courtesy of the Martin and Osa Johnson Safari Museum, Chanute, Kansas. George Eastman photos and photos by unidentified photographers courtesy of the International Museum of Photography at George Eastman House, Rochester, New York, which also generously supplied all photographic prints for this book.

THE *Friends of the University of Rochester Libraries must be com-
mended for the decision to publish* CHRONICLES OF A SECOND
AFRICAN TRIP, *a collection of George Eastman's letters written, and of
photographs taken, during his second trip to Africa in 1928. The publication renews Rochester's long-standing but little known connection to
Africa, a relationship that has taken another step this year with the
establishment at the University of Rochester of the Frederick Douglass
Institute for African and African-American Studies.*

*While Eastman's letters cannot rival the accounts of nineteenth-
century travelers such as Heinrich Barth, Pedroso Gamitto, or David
Livingstone in terms of ethnographic detail, they do raise several issues
pertinent to an understanding of African political economy. They in
particular constitute a compelling testimony to the great changes that the
continent had gone through since the nineteenth century. Whereas Livingstone and his contemporaries could choose what animal to shoot,
Eastman and his party had to go to great lengths to find any animals at
all. The herds had either been exterminated for profit or driven into
reserves, with such serious ecological consequences as the spread of the
tsetse fly and the related sleeping sickness that Eastman described in
the letters.*

*A more remarkable change implicit in the letters concerns the systems
of control that supported the adventures of Eastman and those of his
predecessors. The latter had relied on indigenous political structures for
their safety and for such crucial services as head-porterage. The depen-
dence on African rulers confirmed the prevailing attitudes toward Africans
in some travelers but permitted others to leave the continent with a better
understanding of African realities. Eastman does not appear to have
enjoyed the opportunity for either judgment. He offered neither the ethno-*

centric commonplaces of the one group nor the vivid descriptions of personal acquaintances of the other. His movements were everywhere closely supervised by colonial bureaucrats, eager to please and to explain their enterprise to the famous American visitor. They effectively denied him any meaningful contact with Africans living outside the society of the colonizers.

Many of the photographs taken during the trip have as their background the isolated European communities of district commissioners, medical officers, and merchants. The only Africans to be found in these communities were those who had in different ways been forced to attach themselves to new "outposts of civilization" as laborers. One of Eastman's porters was a man released (temporarily?) from jail, and, like many others, he remains nameless as the "boy" of standard colonial discourse. Others were entertainers who had to perform "native" dances that had lost their context but that satisfied the European sense of the exotic. Nowhere do we see Africans in their daily round of activities, such as farming, cooking, or caring for the elderly and the young.

Similarly, the Neuer conflict with the British in 1928 filtered Eastman's letters through the eyes of the colonial regime: as a "nativistic" rebellion led by the much ill-understood but central figure in African history, the "witch doctor." A people fighting against colonial oppression, like the blacks in South Africa today, thus became, in Eastman's words, a "thorough bad lot [who] may have to be wiped out before the district" can be returned to order. Some of the fruits of the externally imposed order can be seen today in Sudan's ongoing regional conflicts, outbreaks of famine, and the resulting problem of refugees. CHRONICLES OF A SECOND AFRICAN TRIP serves as a valuable guide to the workings and ideology of colonialism at its height during the 1920s.

Eastman's talents as an objective observer show themselves most clearly in the letters written outside the physical and ideological boundaries of the society of the colonizers. The compassion that underlies his unembellished account of meat distribution to a group of starving villagers cannot but inspire admiration for a man who himself never experienced hunger in his adult life. His concern for technical detail, as can be seen in the description of the shadoof (shaduf) device for irrigation on the Nile, provides a glimpse into the mental resourcefulness of the great inventor.

Moreover, unlike the photographs, which for the most part tend to reinforce the colonial view of Africa, these accounts bring to the surface important but unresolved questions about the roots of the agrarian crisis in contemporary Africa.

ELIAS MANDALA
Department of History
University of Rochester
December 1986

INTRODUCTION

GEORGE EASTMAN made his first journey to East Africa in 1926. He was seventy-two and many times a millionaire. Inventor of the inexpensive, popular camera and founder of the Eastman Kodak Company, he was at once a man of great power and of great simplicity. His first hunting safari satisfied both sides of this dichotomy. Combining danger and caution, rigor and civilized comfort, it can be taken as the model of the fully developed safari as laid on by the great companies of Nairobi for wealthy clients. Although Americans had been coming to East Africa for adventure and escape since the 1890s, it had been Theodore Roosevelt's famous trip of 1909 that had shown his countrymen that the British colonies south of Ethiopia and Egypt offered a return to the conditions of the American West before the Civil War—vast herds of game, a land of stunning beauty, a life in the outdoors far from cities.

In 1926, Eastman arrived in Nairobi by private train from Mombasa, as Roosevelt had; Eastman had the best of white hunters, as Roosevelt had; Eastman journeyed widely and shot many animals, as Roosevelt had. Eastman, however, had the advantage of automobiles, in his case specially shipped out from Detroit with their own mechanic; he also took along his own physician. And, like Roosevelt, he was on a partly scientific expedition, collecting specimens for the American Museum of Natural History in New York. Like Roosevelt, he published a book about his experiences, *Chronicles of an African Trip*.

Just when Eastman decided to make a second African trip is unclear. The idea may have had its first stirrings while he was still in Kenya and Tanzania; deeply disappointed by not having shot an elephant, he may have decided even as the first safari ended that he would come back. What is certain is that by March of 1927 he was making firm arrangements for a second trip.

He did not intend to return to Kenya or Tanzania, however. He planned instead to hunt in a tiny area where the Sudan, Uganda, and the then Belgian Congo came together. This area overlapped the Lado Enclave, at the turn of the century the Belgian king's private preserve and for a time after his death the last resort of market ivory hunters, who were for a short while not bothered there by game laws. The region offered two prize animals: the elephant and the white rhinoceros. Despite market hunting, elephants of good size still held on there, and finding one with tusks well above the statutory thirty pounds (per tusk) was likely. The white rhino, on the other hand, was a marginal animal, already prohibited to hunters in most of the areas where it had once flourished because of killing by both hunters and poachers. (The area still includes Uganda's last tiny white rhinoceros enclaves, Mount Kei, Otze Forest, Dufile, and Ajai, but, because of the butchery and poaching following recent upheavals in Uganda, "no White Rhino can now [1981] be found" there.)

Eastman proposed to reach his hunting grounds by steam launch and automobile from Egypt, rather than by safari from East Africa, the more usual route. One newspaper story of the time had him following the route of Kitchener's expedition on the way to its celebrated glories at Omdurman, but the fact is that he followed the Nile, the inevitable water route from Cairo that drills like a borehole into the continent. Leasing a steamer, the *Dal*, through Thomas Cook's, he had it fitted to his taste, including the installation of a refrigerator that figures largely in his account of the trip. The *Dal* would carry him to the limit of navigation at Rejaf (Sudan), where impassable rapids begin (although Gordon had tried to maintain steamers on them fifty years before), and from Rejaf he would make his way by car and truck, the vehicles having been driven overland from Nairobi.

The planning of such a trip was complex, and its expense cannot have been small, nor was Eastman stinting over it: taking along, again, a physician, as well as two guests, he underwrote the costs of probably the best white hunter in British East Africa and a large staff of personal servants, ship's crew, drivers, porters, and many others.

His doctor this time was Albert Kaiser, later chief medical officer of Eastman's home city of Rochester, New York. His guests—replacements for another couple who had earlier hoped to go—were Martin and Osa Johnson, already famous for their films and writings about Borneo and East Africa. The white hunter was Philip Percival, also Eastman's hunter on the first trip. Arguably Kenya's best professional, probably its best known, Percival had worked for Roosevelt and would in 1932 be Ernest Hemingway's hunter and the model for the white hunter in *The Green Hills of Africa.*

Eastman and Kaiser left Rochester on 12 December 1927. They were in Nice, with the Johnsons, for Christmas. Ahead of them lay an extended trip of two thousand miles up the Nile, at the end of which Eastman had scheduled a scant two weeks to bag an elephant and a white rhinoceros.

That journey and its hunts are the subject of this book.

EASTMAN'S life as an outdoorsman began when he was about fifty, fairly late in life but not so late that he missed much of the North American outdoors then available—an outdoors both wilder and less known than ours of today, although much reduced from that of America's pre-industrial age. He hunted and fished rather extensively in North America, taking most of the big game there. Gifted with good health, he roughed it in a day when camping and hunting were far more rigorous than they are now. His invention of camping gadgets showed a desire to improve this primitive state of things— that American desire, in little, that eroded the wildness it celebrated. His collection of camping materials was large and well used, and some of it still exists in boxes he designed, carefully packed by him just before his death.

Not a systematic conservationist, Eastman was nonetheless engaged in the good cause of presenting African wildlife to Americans through Carl Akeley's African Hall at the American Museum of Natural History. Eastman both underwrote part of the Hall's costs and hunted to acquire some of the specimens. Yet, his attitude toward animals was that of the sportsman, not that of the preservationist: animals existed for man's use. The fact that white rhino were endangered (not a concept of the times, in fact) did not deter him from hunting them. The details of a long stalk after a wounded animal, grisly to non-hunters, clearly interested him. As these pages show, he told a hunting story well.

He was not a casual hunter who would leave the real work to his white hunter; despite his age, he wanted to be in at the kill, wanted to make the good shot. He brought good tools to the task: a pair of Westley-Richards .470s for elephant and other large game, three 9.5mm Mannlichers for smaller animals, plus two twenty-gauge Remington shotguns and a pair of Winchester .22s. Clearly, the loss of powers caused by age distressed him—a condition no act of will could change—and much of his enthusiasm for a telescopic sight on one of Osa Johnson's rifles probably came from the improved vision it gave him. Certainly, he seems to have managed to use her gun for most of the trip and to keep it with him when he parted from the Johnsons.

Eastman hunted in the African fashion of the day, with a gunbearer and a white hunter. The gunbearer carried the sportsman's weapon and perhaps another, lighter gun, although gunbearers were themselves forbidden to shoot, except in the rarest of emergencies. (This law, common to most British colonies, dated to the very beginning of the century and has complex roots in racial attitudes, theories of game preservation, and politics.) The white hunter directed the hunt, put out scouts to find the game, managed the stalk if a quarry was seen, and told the sportsman where and when to shoot. The white hunter also carried an appropriate weapon and was ready to fire with or immediately after the sportsman in case of trouble. In case of a kill, the white hunter oversaw the skinning and caping by black craftsmen; in the case of a wounded animal, it was the responsibility of the white hunter to cause his client to finish it—or to pursue the animal and finish it himself, always, with the big animals, a most dangerous task. The expression "white hunter" seems to have first appeared about 1912 and describes a then-new type—the professional hunter, non-African, officially licensed. (Visitors before about 1905 had no Europeans in support but relied on black headmen, gunbearers, and trackers—that is, black hunters.)

For large game—rhino, elephant, buffalo—double-barreled rifles of enormous power were used. The .470 calibre used by Eastman would not have been considered oversize, by far. The two barrels allowed for two almost simultaneous shots, an essential with such huge and unpredictable animals. There were *only* two shots, unfortunately, and a white hunter with courage was a real asset, as a result: he had two more cartridges for the enraged tons of beast that might be charging, even after the second of the sportsman's bullets failed to stop it.

That there was real danger in such hunting is undeniable. It is easy to minimize such danger now, especially if we have never looked down a gun barrel at a wild animal of great size. But men and women were killed and maimed pursuing this sport, and Eastman at seventy-four should be seen as rather remarkable to have taken the risk.

Four years later, he would write the startlingly brief suicide note that would mark the end of his life. Failing in health, he perhaps struck a balance and saw that it was no longer possible to come out ahead. Some may see intimations of that last act in a few of the comments in this book, although there is little here to suggest a man raging against time's inexorable demands. A certain wry regret runs through the pages, but so do authority, courage, and the controlled optimism that governed his life.

THIS account was written as a series of letters, mailed intermittently during the trip, intended for private distribution at home. The letter format was deliberate and allowed Eastman an unvarnished plainness he clearly liked. Even his prose expressed it: clear, undecorated, without metaphor, it allowed for neither fancy nor mystery (the word "mysterious" in letter four is one of the few only partly legible words in the manuscript and may be wrong) and represented the writer—a plain presenter of facts under no compulsion to decorate or entertain. (A Kodak camera, one might say.) This choice of role and the way he exercised it may allow us to see a little what sort of man he was, for the letters are, although cautious and always self-aware, rather informal and, we have to assume, honest.

He was a man of his time, one would say: a theist at best, a rationalist, a materialist, probably a logical positivist. No god is mentioned by him, no intimation of heaven or hell; things are what they are, and they are so presented. Landscape is described, but perhaps more to inform his restricted list of readers than to satisfy any literary urge; what excites him besides his personal enthusiasms (food, hunting, gadgetry) is technology—the squareness of the walls at Abu Simbel, the details of an Egyptian water-raising device, Osa Johnson's new telescopic gunsight. Above all, he was a technophile of the generation that believed that science and machinery would bring the millenium: oil-driven pumps using so much oil would save the labor of so many oxen and so many men; sleeping sickness could be got "in hand" in Uganda by adopting the strict methods used in the Sudan; the problems of the decay of yeast in a hot climate could be solved by adopting his method of sterilization and sterile storage.

He was a man with a sense of humor. We encounter a sly, self-derogatory wit, as when he writes of the improvised sedan chair on which he was carried "like some Indian potentate with an umbrella;" "if we come up with an elephant I suppose I may have to stand up to shoot." There is a hint of laughter, too, in the description of a boring part of the trip as "not distinctly uncomfortable," which has the ring of a running gag, perhaps an old George Eastman line.

He was a man who liked certain comforts and certain pleasures. Champagne was one; "Pommery Sec" was a feature of the journey. He liked good food, especially good breads and biscuits: Eastman's enthusiasm for cooking is well documented. He was a dedicated camp cook and an inventor of outdoor cooking contrivances, including a portable stove; his "wheat gems" (a kind of graham whole wheat flour) and his "mixtures" (packaged mixes before supermarkets carried them) figure often in his account.

He was an unmarried man who liked attractive women. When at home in Rochester, he entertained four young married women each week. In Osa Johnson, he found a good companion—a lively, bright, interesting woman, and one with whom he had spent a good deal of time on his first trip. (One of the most touching photos of them together is one published in the Johnsons' books, showing Osa and Eastman bending over a bush campfire where they are baking bread.) In the hundreds of photographs her husband took of her, we see a woman who always smiled, one perhaps like the idealized heroines of the Chaplin one-reelers—plucky, pretty, determinedly feminine. Eastman liked her; most men liked her. And she could shoot, cook, and bushwhack with the best of them. As Eastman himself wrote, "Osa has about all the [game animal] trophies."

Osa Johnson was married to a man whose work Eastman respected and had underwritten, for Eastman was one of those who had supported Martin Johnson's animal photography for several years while the Johnsons lived at their "Lake Paradise," a volcanic crater on the mountain oasis of Marsabit, Kenya. However, it is Osa and not Martin who appears constantly in these pages. Martin is seen only rarely, worth mentioning for his lumbago or his camera work.

Eastman seems in these pages a man who, in Anthony Powell's words, "lived by the will," one who formed his world to his own needs, one who got his money's worth. One senses this quality in his hunting most of all: he wants an elephant; he gives himself two weeks and gets an elephant. He wants a white rhino, on the last license granted in Africa; he gets one. This is the exercise of will, indomitable despite his age. His white hunter tells him there are not many men his age who will do what he has done.

He seems a man who exercised power in subtle ways but exercised it pervasively. His was the double stateroom on the *Dal*, although the Johnsons were a couple and had to sleep in separate rooms. He took the middle of three houses in a camp (and the only one with a porch). He took the only chance at a white rhino, the first and perhaps only chance at an elephant. It was his trip, after all.

And Eastman responded to Africa like a man of his time, "restricted to experiencing Africa solely on [his] own terms," as a modern historian has put it. We cannot expect more of him. Africans were "natives" or "boys"; of the hundreds who worked for him on this journey, none had a name he bothered to record. One was described by him as "intelligent for a native." The Neuers, a Sudanese tribe who had given the British trouble, were a "thorough bad lot and may have to be wiped out." "Witch doctor" and "chief" were useful terms. Behind his words was the racism of the day, so deep and so

[*xxiii*]

accepted as to seem part of the natural scheme of things. Indeed, his stated racial ideas were less harsh than Roosevelt's, in fact less so than those of most whites of the time.

THE letters that make up this account were addressed to his secretary, Alice Whitney Hutchison. That this arrangement was a convenient fiction seems clear from the fact that, as letter ten shows, Eastman knew that she had left the country during the time he was writing. And, as other references show, these letters were to be duplicated in Rochester and distributed—"published"—to a small group of friends. ("Of course Mrs. Kaiser is on the list to receive copy of letters," says a note on one, apparently added by Eastman in answer to a query.)

The originals of these pages are sixty-one ruled sheets, written on in pencil. The body of the account was written without change, whether from another draft or not is unknown, although the presence of minor changes in the same hand suggests that this is the first draft. Revisions and interlineations are minor and consist of corrections (time of day, place, and so on) and small additions, usually to provide more detail. It is not clear, however, that Eastman wrote this account for publication beyond the limited circulation of typed copies. What is certain is that he did not publish it as a book during his lifetime, although it was written very much as *Chronicles of an African Trip* had been. The hand-written pages have been for some time in the collection of the Department of Rare Books and Special Collections in the University of Rochester library, where I found them in 1984 while looking for material on the Johnsons. They had probably been ignored before this because their file label made them seem the manuscript of the record of the first African trip.

The similarities between his writing of the accounts of the two African journeys suggest that he may have intended another book, at least at first. On the other hand, his response to publication of *Chronicles of an African Trip* was not always positive. Published privately, that book was distributed as a gift to friends, acquaintances, and Kodak employees. (A file in the University of Rochester library is stuffed with thank-you notes for gift copies, one letter signed by dozens of French Kodak employees. What can they have made of this English account of an Africa that was not even French?) Perhaps experience with the first book led him to believe that a second was unwise.

It is certain that Eastman wrote these pages to be transcribed and corrected. A note added to one letter assumed that it would be edited, presumably by his secretary. A typed and edited version of one letter exists and is filed with the manuscript. Minor corrections to the handwritten text were needed: he wrote with little punctuation and many abbreviations; like technocrats today, he may have believed that "writing" and its finer points were things that other people could be paid to do.

In preparing the manuscript for publication, I have tried to use the standard (although not the editorial style) of *Chronicles of an African Trip* as a guide, aiming at readability rather than strict reproduction of Eastman's manuscript. As a result, this is not a scholarly edition: it does not attempt to reproduce his spellings, his punctuation, his corrections, or any of the idiosyncracies of the pencilled manuscript. A very few changes have been made in the words themselves where greater clarity was needed ("that" for "which" where appropriate; substitution of the noun for a pronoun). I have normalized spelling and punctuation to modern standards ("stayed" for the manuscript "staid", for example; the serial comma; "seven" for "7," and so on). It is in punctuation that the most work had to be done; Eastman wrote complex sentences with clauses added one after another and frequent parenthetical material, usually without any commas at all. I have tried to punctuate sparingly, using an open rather than a closed model.

Explanatory notes will be found at the end of the letters, keyed by page rather than by a footnote number. Again, I decided at the outset to forego footnotes, brackets, or interpolations in the name of readability. I hope it has been achieved.

KENNETH M. CAMERON
Washington, DC
December 1986

CHRONICLES OF A SECOND AFRICAN TRIP

1. Setting Sail. Eastman, Osa Johnson,
and Dr. Kaiser on the transatlantic crossing.
(*Martin Johnson photo.*)

December 26, 1927

HOTEL RUHL
NICE

Dear Mrs. Hutchison,

Here we are at Nice, looking out on a sullen surf roaring on the beach in front of our hotel. There is a slight mist, and altogether the prospect is far from what is expected in this land of alleged sunshine. In fact, we haven't seen much sunshine since we left Rochester. The voyage was not uncomfortably rough, but the beds on the *Beringaria* were the worst ever and contributed a good deal to the sleeplessness that I had been suffering since the first week at Oak Lodge.

The weather in Paris was rainy all the time and I hardly left the Hotel Plaza except to go to the office and to see the new shop in the Place Vendôme. The latter is very attractive, and although it is in the prevailing modern style it is not offensively so. The general effect is very spacious and bright. The location is absolutely the best in Paris, and I think the purchase of the property was quite a stroke in our favor. The building still has scaffolding on the side entrance, and the upper part will not be finished until April.

On Thursday, Lord Riddell, Albert Levy, Sir Frank Newnes, and Secretary Garret of the Royal Free Hospital came to the hotel and we fixed up an agreement by which I turned over two hundred thousand pounds to a committee consisting of Riddell, Levy, and Mattison so they could let the contract during my absence, relieving me of all further responsibility, the plans drawn by Sir John Burnet and partners having been previously approved by Dr. Burkhart and me.

We left Paris about eight o'clock Saturday night on one of the half-dozen special holiday trains and arrived here at 1:30 P.M. yesterday, Christmas day. In the evening, we all dined with Mr. and Mrs. Bouveng, Florence, and Miss Foster, Mrs. Bouveng's sister, at their hotel, the Angleterre, in the next block. It was a gala night, with a big Christmas tree in the balcony, a dancing floor in the center, and much champagne. I stayed until after ten and then slipped out. For some reason or other—perhaps it was the champagne—I had the best sleep I have had in a month (about six hours straight) and felt much refreshed this morning. At the present rate, I shall be quite all right before I get to Rejaf, and maybe by the time we get to Khartoum.

This afternoon, we are all going in a bus along the lower road to Monte Carlo (forty-five minutes). Osa is crazy to try her luck. Al has been there, but as it was during the war and he was in uniform he did not get into the Casino. We leave tomorrow noon for Genoa (five or six hours), spend the next day there, and sail the twenty-ninth in the *Italia* for Alexandria, arriving January second at 2:00 P.M.

Ever yours,
G E

Cairo, *January* 4, 1928

Dear Mrs. Hutchison,

Monday afternoon (December 26), the four of us with Mr. Bouveng went over to Monte Carlo in the motor bus—about three-quarters of an hour's ride. It was raining most of the time, and the place did not have its usual gay aspect. On the way over, I took some pains to explain to Osa the hopelessness of expecting to win money at the game: that, while it was perfectly straight, the odds in favor of the bank are so heavy that if one played long enough he was absolutely sure to lose. I told her that it was managed by an incorporated English stock company that published its accounts every year, and that its profits did not depend upon luck at all but solely upon the amount of its turnover. She listened patiently, but I could see that she was not much impressed.

As soon as we got into the roulette room, she made Martin buy her some checks and began to test her luck. We had about an hour and a half before our bus started back, and so I found a comfortable chair in the outer room and sat down to smoke the time away. When Bouveng rounded up the party to go home, we found that Osa had had a run of luck, and although she was playing with only 5-franc pieces she had won about 560 francs, while Martin had lost about 100. The two were 460 to the good. In one case, she had insisted on betting on the seven and had won thirty-five to one, at which she was so excited that it made all the people at her end of the table laugh—quite an unusual thing in that solemn place. You can imagine the scorn with which she referred to my mathematical advice.

The next day, we left for Genoa after calling to say goodbye to Mrs. Bouveng, Miss Foster, and Florence. The train was very luxurious and fast. We had luncheon aboard and arrived at Genoa in time for a late dinner at the Miramare, the big hotel on the hill. The

Kodak manager, Mr. Ballerini, met us at the station and took dinner with us. The next day, I stayed most of the time in the hotel, only visiting the office for a few minutes. In the evening, we went to the opera but stayed for only the first act, as it was very dull. We had a box in the middle of the horseshoe next to the royal box, but that did not help any, as the king was not there. The opera house has six tiers of boxes and looks like a pigeon coop and is about as comfortable, I should think.

The next day at eleven, we sailed for Naples on the *Italia* (seven thousand tons) en route to Alexandria. It was the only bright day since we left Rochester and the sun was welcome, although I can't say that I object especially to cloudy weather. At Naples we had all day for sightseeing, but after visiting our shop, which was new to me, and taking lunch with the others at a restaurant, I returned to the ship. The others did a little sightseeing.

We had a smooth and uneventful voyage and landed at Alexandria after luncheon. Our baggage took so much time that we had to take the 7:00 P.M. train for Cairo, having dinner on the train. They made us open the tin-lined box containing the guns, for purposes of identification. As soon as we got to Cairo, I took a hot bath and got into a very comfortable bed at "Shepheards", which, by the way, is not nearly so swagger a place as I supposed. The season is just opening and it is only about half full, which of course is always an advantage in traveling. Cooks and the Sudan government officials were very obliging, and we had no difficulty in arranging for our twenty pieces of heavy luggage (including, of course, the Johnsons'). Mr. Nassibian was very attentive and drove us out to the pyramids the morning of the day we left and also showed us his sister's house on the return road. The husband was an antiquarian, and the house is a regular museum of old Turkish work, besides being built in the Turkish style.

We are taking train for Khartoum at six-thirty. Everything lovely so far.

Yours truly,
G E

Sunday, January 8, 1928

Dear Mrs. Hutchison,

The journey by rail from Cairo at 6:30 P. M. Wednesday (just three weeks from New York) to Shellal at noon Thursday was uneventful and not very interesting—it was dark most of the way. The train was what they call "deluxe," which means equal to average Pullman. At Shellal (Assuan), we transferred to a small stern-paddlewheel steamer, on which we spent a day and a half and two nights going the length of the backwater formed by the big dam. This passage was through rocky hills with occasional narrow strips along the sides irrigated by means of shadufs, one-man water-lifters having a pole pivoted above the bank, weighted at one end with a rock and at the other with a rope and a bucket. A native, standing so his waist is about the level of the bank, pulls down the bucket, which fills itself in the river; then he pulls it up and tips it over into the little irrigation trench on the bank. I timed several and they made twelve lifts per minute.

Another contrivance is worked by two cows or bullocks that draw a pole around a vertical shaft having a horizontal shaft geared to it with wood teeth. The outside end of the horizontal shaft carries a rope rigging long enough to reach down to the river and having a series of buckets that empty themselves into the ditch as they go over the shaft. Both contrivances are as old as history and of course highly inefficient. It takes nearly all they can grow to feed either the one man or the two oxen.

We came up on the train from Wadi Halfa last night with a government official who said his mission to Khartoum was to get the government to make an appropriation of two thousand pounds to buy some small pumping outfits that use crude oil, and to make a demonstration that one of them, using oil costing as much as the feed for two oxen, would pump more water than ten pairs—and of course save the labor of nine men besides.

On the way up the river about nine o'clock Friday night we stopped to look at the temple of Abu Simbel. A most remarkable work, carved in the side of a sloping bluff. Four enormous sitting figures 65 feet high are carved on the face of the rock, and between them is a doorway, I should think 8 or 10 by 30 feet, which leads to a series of lofty rooms extending into the rock perhaps 150 feet. One of the chambers is supported by rows of giant, detached standing figures on each side. The walls are cut true and vertical and the ceilings flat. On the ceilings are frescoes in dull colors, and hieroglyphics are carved on the walls. This temple impressed me more than the pyramids.

At Wadi Halfa we transferred to the Sudan Railway Train, a really tropical affair having double roofs and blue "sun-proof" glass, which lessens the glare of the sun and does not obstruct the view. These precautions must be very helpful in summer, but just now the weather is perfectly delightful, ranging from 58 degrees Fahrenheit at night to 77 at midday. (They say it reaches 115 degrees in summer.)

On the train I received a wire from the High Commissioner to Egypt saying he had missed me at Cairo but had wired the Governor General of the Sudan at Khartoum to do anything he could for me on our arrival there. All along the way, officials have been very attentive and polite, and we are not suffering for anything. One official wired to Albara about our General Electric refrigerator, and we had an answer at breakfast on the train this morning that it had been set up on the *Dal* and was in working order. After we got settled at the hotel, another official took us across the river in a launch to the dock where the *Dal* is being fitted for the trip, and the company engineer who had installed the refrigerator said it made the trays full of ice in four hours.

Our ammunition and guns came through with no trouble, except for a little red tape, and now everything seems set for our departure three days ahead of time. This will give us three more precious days for shooting on the way up.

We inspected some "headmen" at the Sudan office and selected one who looked capable (not handsome), who speaks four or five

2. Egyptian-Sudanese Train.
En route to Khartoum, probably taken at Wadi Halfa.
(*George Eastman photo.*)

languages, and who has had great experience in handling his fellow natives. He is tall and has a fierce military bearing that is quite impressive. We also visited the game warden and made arrangements for our licenses. He gave us a lot of information about the game along the way and said the season is all in our favor because the river is about two meters lower than usual at this time of year, which dryness drives the game down toward the river.

I have nothing to worry me now except the butter. We had rancid butter at the hotel for luncheon, which doesn't look promising for the *Dal* supply. Wouldn't it be a joke on us if after all our trouble to bring along our nice biscuit mixtures we should have to use rancid butter on them?

Khartoum is a most attractive place. To all appearances it is a new city, with broad streets and vast spaces for every requirement. Many of the private places are walled in with low walls having iron fences on top. The governor's palace and the Grand Hotel, where we are stopping, front on a grand boulevard skirting the Blue Nile. This boulevard has a fine embankment about twenty-five feet high on the riverside, and there is a lovely view across the river, where Omdurman lies.

Tuesday, January 10. Yesterday afternoon we went over to Omdurman, the native city, in a taxi and on the ferry. A bridge is finished and will be opened next week, but we had to use the ferry. We drove around the town (natives only), which stretches about six miles along the river. Saw the Mahdi's house, the place where he was buried until the body was dug up and burned by the authorities and the ashes thrown in the river to prevent the natives' making a shrine of the place. We also drove out to the edge of the town where we could see the Kitchener battlefield.

The town is a vast conglomeration of one-story mud buildings having walls next to the street and courtyards within. The shallow shops, of course, face the street and are open on that side. Not a blade of grass anywhere—only dust the color of the mud walls. Recently, electricity has been meagerly installed, and a trolley line will run over the new bridge to Khartoum, where only the white people live.

3 and 4. Crew Members of the *Dal*.
Eastman snapped these pictures
and mailed them home;
they were distributed with the
typed letters to friends.
(*George Eastman photos.*)

An investigation of the supplies from the boat reveals that we are to have fresh Australian butter of first-class quality and that the rancid (?) butter at the hotel was an accident, so at present we cannot find anything to worry about.

The boat, with its barge (which is nearly as big as the *Dal*) lashed alongside, was brought up to the steps in front of the hotel at nine o'clock this morning. It has all its equipment in place and everything looks shipshape and comfortable. I have double rooms opening together across the rear of the deck house. Osa and Al have corner rooms forward, and Martin has a room next to Osa's and an extra room for a laboratory. There is a bathroom and toilet room for the Johnsons and a set for Al and me, all in the one deck. Still farther forward is a very pleasant dining room, and at the bow, opening from the dining room, is an open space for canvas chairs. The food is all brought up the main stairway, between the bedroom deckhouse and the dining room. The crew, donkeys, camp equipment, and heavy baggage are provided for on the barge alongside.

I am writing this at the Grand Hotel, which is owned and run by the Sudan government, which apparently runs everything here very efficiently. It is of course a bright summer's day, with a lovely breeze, and I am still wearing at ten o'clock a light jersey under the sack coat that I put on at breakfast.

They say this good weather continues until sometime in April. Then, until September, extreme heat, insects, and sandstorms combine to make the place a veritable hell on earth.

Yours truly,
G E

5. At the Khartoum Zoo. Although not mentioned in the letters,
a trip to the Khartoum zoo was made by Eastman and Osa,
as indicated by the captions on proofs of photos in the University of
Rochester library. Here, Osa with a baby elephant.
(*George Eastman photo.*)

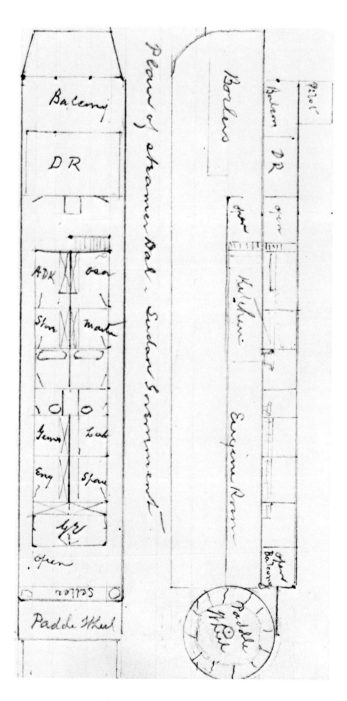

6. Eastman's Floor Plan of the *Dal*.

January 11, 1928

Dear Mrs. Hutchison,

If the past twenty-four hours is a fair sample of what we are to expect between Khartoum and Rejaf, I can see that I am to be a disappointed man. To tell the truth, I did not expect it to be a very comfortable trip, especially compared to the one in British East Africa, so you can imagine how I feel when I say that I never spent a more satisfactory twenty-four hours on any trip.

In the first place, the *Dal* is perfectly lovely now that it is all furnished up with new furniture, linens, tableware, and kitchen outfit. The forward deckhouse begins with a balcony about six feet wide across the front, on which there are a small circular table and some canvas reclining chairs, which are really comfortable. Then comes the dining room—fifteen feet wide and ten feet deep—with windows on the sides and doors fore and aft so the breeze can blow through. Then comes a cross passage fifteen feet long, all open across the ship, in which is the main companionway, then a deckhouse about thirteen feet wide with a row of five staterooms and a bath and a toilet room on each side.

The Johnsons occupy the starboard side, except one room that is vacant. Kaiser has the corner room forward next to the staircase on the port side; then there is a vacant bedroom (except that it is used as a storeroom), then a bath and toilet, then the bedroom (which we use as a gun room), and then the engineer's room. Then my two rooms, which occupy the space across the deck house aft and by sliding doors make practically one large room with two beds, one of which I use as a table for my suitcases. Then a space about eight feet wide across the stern upon which the doors of my apartment open, with rugs and chairs and a table. All around the boat are canvas curtains that can be let down to keep out the sun.

There are two cooks and a scullery boy. The chief cook is quite an artist, and all we have to do is curb him lest he overfeed us. There are two waiters and two cabin boys. The boat is in charge of the engineer, who has three assistants. There is a pilot with two assistants. The headwaiter has charge of the cuisine and has fifty pounds provided by the government commissary department to buy chickens, eggs, and so on from the natives when he can get them.

The butter is all right. We have in the refrigerator thirty pounds of it that is nice and sweet, straight from Australia. By the way, we did not discover until about six o'clock last night that the engineer (who is a Sudanese who does not speak English) had not started the refrigerator. He had been taught to run it but thought we needed to run it only when we wanted to make ice cubes. It took hours to get everything stored in it cold, but it works like a charm and is going to be a great treasure.

We passed under the new bridge just above Khartoum about 3:00 P.M. and then felt we were fully started. The banks are flat, and strips along the shore are cultivated, being watered by shadufs and an occasional sakiyeh. There are strings of mimosa trees, which look like apple trees, scattered along, relieving the monotony of the skyline.

Before sunset, we began to see crocodiles on the bank and a few hippo, the latter always swimming in the river. The moon rose about nine o'clock—three days on the wane, which in this latitude flattens it on the top, making it look egg shaped. It was still big enough to make a splendid moonlight night.

After an elaborate and excellent dinner that ended with a cup of Turkish coffee, it certainly was the height of luxury to loll in our comfortable chairs and watch the river and the mysterious landscape glide by.

The morning after we left Khartoum, two biplanes sailed by, coming from the south and heading for Khartoum. They were very likely part of an operation against the natives who murdered Ferguson, the government agent, just beyond Rejaf. We heard that the government is going to bomb their villages and teach them a lesson. The place is along our road, but of course we will not be allowed to stop there.

7. The *Dal.* Rented and outfitted for Eastman
by Thomas Cook's, the boat had a companion barge (closer to the camera)
for crew, livestock, and supplies. Members of Eastman's party
are on the roof of the wheelhouse.
(*Martin Johnson photo.*)

Friday evening, January 13. Ever since the first day, we have been seeing "crocs" along the banks of the river and hippos in the water. The hippos show only their heads, as a rule. We are not allowed to shoot anything from the boat except crocs, and we occasionally practice on them. As a rule, they jump or roll into the water, but today Osa killed one dead with her new .30 Springfield with telescope sight. She is very keen over this rifle, which was given her by Griffin and Howe of New York at the suggestion of Dick Burkhart. The sight magnifies the object two and a half times and permits one to see the whole image. It is the best one I have ever seen, and I shall have to have one fitted to my Mannlicher, which I prefer to the Springfield. The telescope is placed above the ordinary sight and does not interfere with its use. [A drawing of the sight as seen through the eyepiece was included here.]

January 14. This morning at six-thirty, Al and I went ashore to try and get roan antelope. After about an hour and a half on our nice little donkeys, we saw two good specimens. Just before we got into shooting range, a small antelope about the size of an East African Tommy popped up in the grass and frightened them away. To pay him for his butting in, I dropped him with my Mannlicher. As this was my first time out, I thought I would not overdo, so I came back to the boat with my donkey boy, two of the shikaris carrying the game, while Al went after the roan. He came up with them again but failed to get one, as he has not got used to his rifle yet.

Just now, at noon, we are tied up to the bank putting on wood. We started out from Khartoum with coal, but wood is the regular fuel and we have to stop at least every two days to load up. The government has wood piles at various places, and loading up takes three or four hours. They are evidently experimenting with Diesel engines, for the next boat to this one in the dockyard at Khartoum had one on it, but the superintendent told us the gear had been giving trouble and the Diesel was not in use.

8. Osa and Dr. Kaiser on the *Dal*.
The rifle leaning against the chair appears to be Osa's Springfield.
(*Martin Johnson photo.*)

While I have been writing this, a steamboat has pulled up to our woodpile, and if it carries mail I will put this aboard.

Yours,
Geo Eastman

["Sheet xx" followed: Eastman's plan and cross-section of the *Dal*, as well as a list of personnel, as follows.]

The following is a full list of the personnel:

1 pilot
2 2nd pilots
1 engineer
1 2nd engineer
2 assistants
14 "sailors" and firemen
1 barge sailor
3 donkey boys
6 gunbearers and tent boys
————
31

3 cooks
2 waiters
2 cabin boys
————
38 total men

Five saddle donkeys and 10 pack donkeys on the barge alongside. There are also coops containing live pigeons, chickens, and turkeys.

9. A Stop on the Nile. The *Dal* and its barge
at a dock with an unidentified boat. At such stops, firewood
and food supplies were taken on and mail was exchanged.
(*George Eastman photo.*)

10. A Dinka Village on the Nile.
(*Martin Johnson photo.*)

January 16, 1928

Above Malakal:
The River Nile and the Steamer *Dal*

Dear Mrs. Hutchison,

This is the sixth day since leaving Khartoum, and we are just half-way to Rejaf. To this point, the river is practically a straight line. Here it makes a big bend to the east and there is nearly a straight line again to Rejaf; of course there are short curves everywhere, but you can usually see up and down for a mile or two. The country on either side is perfectly flat, and since the second day we have seen very little cultivation on the banks. There is instead a strip of green rushes thirty or forty yeards wide where the cultivated ground was, and for the last two days only a few trees—just a brown, grassy plain that has been burned off in patches. As we go along at night we can see fires burning at intervals, sometimes three or four at a time.

Every few miles there are native villages of straw huts with pointed roofs, and small herds of cattle and goats. The natives, at least the men and children, are usually naked. The women apparently stay in the huts unless they are carrying water from the river, and then they have a dirty cloth draped over their shoulders and hips.

Yesterday noon (Sunday) we stopped at *Kodok*. It is a post office with a native police station and what amounts to two villages—one near the river bank and the other half a mile farther back near the post office, where there are a barracks, an office building, and some brick houses for the school teachers—all natives. We all bought some post-cards and got the postmaster to postmark them plainly, as souvenirs.

Martin got some interesting pictures, in some of which appears a sign I made on a strip of canvas taken from one of our reclining deck chairs. The tools employed were a dinner and a dessert plate to get the curves, a phonograph record envelope to get the straight lines and angles, and a couple of carpenter's pencils with heavy black lead to "ink in" between the outlines.

Al examined a group of children for their teeth, adenoids, and tonsils, and Martin picked out a native with a remarkable headdress who was about six feet six inches high and who must have been a chief and called him "King of Kodok" and made a picture of him to go along with mine and the sign, to be entitled "the Kodak King at Kodok."

Tuesday, January 17. The river split just before we got to the bend, and we went up the narrow branch about half a mile to a wood pile to load up, for there is a long stretch of the Sudd, or swampy ground, where there is no wood. We tied up about sunset, and while loading we had a fine view of the western bank, which for a distance of about two miles was being burned off. The fire was about half a mile or a mile back from the river, and between it and the river near the fire was a fringe of trees, which, as I said before, look like apple trees. Viewed from the top, or roof, deck, the fire showed under the trees, and the flames did not rise above them except in short flashes. The smoke, lighted by the fire behind the trees, rose in a long white cloud and floated lazily along parallel to the river, making a magnificent spectacle. We drew out about ten and left the "fireworks" with much regret.

We have seen very little game so far. Night before last about sundown, too late to go ashore, we saw a few gazelle and waterbuck, but nothing important. Just now we are in perhaps the least interesting part of the river, because the swampy banks are covered with papyrus that is too dense and high for any game to show if any were there.

Between Shambe and Bor, a little farther up the river, is where the government is conducting operations against the tribe that killed Ferguson and his companions, and we will not be allowed to go ashore, I understand. There is another place farther back where a witch doctor is trying to stir up trouble, but our route does not take us very near the seat of that trouble.

While I was writing this, Osa called me to try her new gun on a croc lying on the surface of the water. That telescope sight is certainly fine.

Life on the *Dal* is very luxurious. Even when it is hottest (in the early afternoon), when the thermometer registers 102 degrees (which is the hottest so far), a comfortable spot can be found where there is a little breeze on the bow or stern balcony. There have been no flies or

11. The Kodak King at Kodok With His Kodak.
Eastman made the sign himself, captivated by a village name
so like that of his company. He holds the Kodak camera
with which he took many of these pictures.
(*Martin Johnson photo.*)

12. In the Sudd. Until the twentieth century,
this "green prison" often blocked the Nile completely.
(*Martin Johnson photo.*)

mosquitoes so far, and we have not had to sleep under the nets. Osa and Martin have elected to have cots placed in the screened house on the top deck, while Al and I have found it perfectly comfortable in our corner rooms, which have windows on two sides.

Thanks to the General Electric refrigerator, the cuisine is getting on splendidly. Night before last I started to make a mince pie but found that the crust mixture was so soft in the can that it couldn't be handled, so I put it in the refrigerator. Last night it had got so hard I had to cut it out with a table knife. After I crumbled it up and added the water it worked all right.

Here are some typical menus:

Breakfast—Fresh grapefruit (while it lasts. We have loads of canned grapefruit, which, because it is ice cold, everybody likes as well as the fresh.) Quaker Oats with super cream, bacon and eggs or kippered herring or smoked halibut, corn meal or wheat gems from GE mixtures. GE coffee.

Luncheon—Hors d'oeuvres, iced ship's coffee, toast, wild duck, potatoes, canned string beans or, say, curried rice, jellied canned mixed fruits.

Dinner—Cocktails, soup, breast of wild guinea hen, vegetables, soda biscuit, Pommery Sec, lemon tarts, mince or huckleberry pie or Eliza's suet pudding with foaming sauce. Turkish coffee. Music from the phonograph.

The cook—I suppose we ought to call him chef (see picture)—is quite an artist on hors d'oeuvres and makes some attractive platters of them for luncheon.

So much for the purely material side. Between meals we read, study the map, watch for crocs, hippos, and birds (of which latter there is a great variety), and take hot baths. It doesn't look to me as if I would ever be willing to do any more work.

The six shikaris (or gunbearers, skinners, and gametrackers), whom we took on at Rink, camp by themselves at the bow of the barge just off our front porch and furnish us something of interest in watching their mode of life. They, or most of them, are Moham-medans and perform their genuflections at sunset every evening.

Up to this evening, we have had no flies or mosquitoes, but about four o'clock we tied up to the bank to get some grass for the donkeys and sheep, and since then there has been a perfect cloud of midges, so we have to keep within the screened area.

We have seen several elephants today, one very large one about a mile out on the plain beyond the papyrus grass and traveling away from the river, so he was out of reach. We hope in a few days to get where we can get a shot at one, but that will be pure luck if we do.

Wednesday, January 18. We are still in the Sudd, and it is getting monotonous, although not distinctly uncomfortable. The midges bothered us only two or three hours, and since then we have been free from insects, although we have fifteen donkeys and half a dozen goats on the lower deck of the barge. Owing to the fact that it is all open, there is no smell from them (or the deck hands).

We expect to meet a mail boat some time this evening, so I will close this. No bugs or mosquitoes yet. Temperature after dinner eighty-two degrees in my room.

Yours,

G E

13. Wheelhouse of the *Dal*.
(*Martin Johnson photo.*)

14. Eastman With Crocodile.
He has just shot the animal with Osa's gun.
(*George Eastman photo.*)

January 19, 1928

Dear Mrs. Hutchison,

Osa called me again this morning to try her gun on a big croc floating on the surface near the bank of the Sudd. I fired when we were within sixty to eighty yards and he never moved. The croc was in shallow water, so they nosed the *Dal* as near as possible, and two boys went overboard and hitched a rope around his middle, and the boys on the bow hauled him aboard, and although he was only nine feet four inches long we decided to save his skin, so the skinners went at it. Working by turns, three or four of them took several hours to skin him and cut him up. They saved everything but the skeleton. Some of them wanted the meat and fat, but others would not touch it.

At two o'clock, we got to Shambe, the headquarters of the military operations against the Neuers, the rebellious tribe that killed Ferguson about ten days ago. There is a wood station there, so we stayed three hours to fill up. There was no evidence of war there, except a few military tents set up as a hospital. There is quite a native town and a garage with some trucks. The real seat of operations is inland about thirty miles west. They have got the whole Neuer tribe, said to be nearly ten thousand, bottled up in the swamp; they have destroyed their cattle and villages, and the orders are, it is said, to clean them out, as they are a hopeless lot influenced by some witch doctor. Two nights ago, some of them raided the town where we were and speared ten men near the edge of the town, killing two. One of the wounded, with a spear hole in his chest, was in the hospital, where Al saw him this afternoon.

The local tribe, Dinkas, are a peaceable tribe and much worked up over the situation. They are a poor lot—100 percent syphilitic, the local doctor, an Armenian, said. By the way, this doctor has a brother keeping a restaurant on Exchange Street, and he was much interested when he heard we were from Rochester, he having been there himself last summer. He was educated at Beirut.

During the day, ten bombing planes had arrived from Khartoum, and they are looking for decisive action in the next few days.

January 20. Began to see elephants in the grass at 9:00 A.M. By ten o'clock had seen at least fifty, and during the day more than a hundred, some even quite near the river, and one herd of about twenty were quite angry and would have charged the boat if they could have got at it. All they could do was to lift their trunks and trumpet their opinion of us. We saw only one bull that had good ivory, but if they all had been good specimens we could not have touched them, as we are not allowed to shoot from the boat, and the marsh is so wet and the grass so high that it would be impossible to see one if we got ashore. We could see them only from the top deck, so we had to go along.

We did not get to the end of the Sudd until we reached Bor. We stopped and tied up at about 11:00 P.M., three hours beyond Bor, and this morning at six-thirty, after a hurried breakfast, we set out on our donkeys to see if we could find anything. After traveling an hour and a half inland at a smart walk, we found nothing and started on a circle toward the boat. We soon began to see a few gazelles, and I shot at a small one about the size of a Tommy, and afterwards at a larger one, a good roan, but missed them both as they were so far away. Then Al got a very good waterbuck with twenty-nine-inch horns. It took an hour to skin the head and cut up the meat for the boys (it is too tough for our table), and so it was about eleven-thirty when we got back to the *Dal*. Fortunately it was cloudy (even just a sprinkle of rain about ten o'clock) with a nice breeze, so we were not overheated. When we got back, we found that our pack donkeys, which had been let out on the veldt to get a little grass, had run away, so instead of staying tied up to the bank in the broiling sun, we started up the river to see if we could see any elephants, leaving a couple of the boys to round up seven donkeys that were still out. We had not been under way more than an hour before we began to pick up a lot of elephants in the now open fields, some right among the native cattle. Now, at three-thirty,

15. Hunting on the Nile Shores. Eastman was concerned
about his stamina but did very well; he had often ridden both mules
and horses on his North American trips.
(*George Eastman photo.*)

we have seen over a hundred, and on our way back to pick up the donkeys we shall probably tie up at the likeliest spot for a hunt this afternoon or early tomorrow morning.

We did not see a single elephant on our way back to the landing place that would do to shoot. On getting back after dark, we found there were still seven donkeys missing, so we left word with the head native to continue searching and we would pick them up when we came back down the river from Rejaf.

We went on up the river and arrived early at a wood station. We decided that while taking on wood we would go out looking for game, so we put up some luncheon and water and started out about nine-thirty. It was an hour and a half before we came up with anything. Finally, we saw a small herd of roan, and my gunbearer and I started after them on foot. I finally got a shot but hit him about a foot too far back, and he went on. We followed him as far as I could and then gave him up reluctantly. I was pleased, though, that I could do a mile and a half or two miles on foot in the hot sun so well. Afterward, Al got a tiang (which is almost exactly like a topi, of which I brought home the skins of eight or ten from B.E.A.). We had our luncheon under a tree and got back about 4:00 P.M. After a good bath and some iced tea we all felt fresh as daisies. We are now at Mongalla, and after breakfast we are going to call on the assistant governor of the province.

After seeing the assistant, or deputy, governor, we have decided to go on to Rejaf, where we hope to find permits to take our two gunbearers and three tent boys along with us to Uganda. Phil has arranged for all the rest.

This will be put on the mail boat for Khartoum, which will pause here at 11:00 A.M.

Everything okay up to this point, but little game so far.

Yours,
G E

16. Eastman's Gunbearer.
(*Martin Johnson photo.*)

17. Motor Safari. At Rejaf, the party left the *Dal*
and was met by the vehicles for the journey to White Rhino Camp.
(*George Eastman photo*).

January 26, 1928

Yei, Sudan (pronounced yay)

Dear Mrs. Hutchison,

We arrived at this place with our two cars and two trucks about six-thirty last evening, having left Rejaf right after luncheon. All feeling well except Osa, who had been troubled with dysentery for two days. She had not said anything to the doctor about it, but when it came to starting out, she felt so miserable that a council of war had to be called. It was finally decided to get as far as Arua if we could. In fact, we did not know whether we could do even that, even if she were well, because we had been unable to get permission to carry our three personal servants and two gunbearers, needed for the hunt, across the border.

Yei is the headquarters for the Sudan border medical service, and they are trying desperately to keep out the sleeping sickness, which is more or less rampant in the Belgian Congo. The first man we saw when we arrived (at sunset) was the district physician-in-charge, and after some talk he invited us to camp on his porch. This proved a godsend because Osa had to go to bed right away.

It took only a few minutes to unload and set up her bed, and she was made very comfortable, with two doctors in attendance. The head doctor returned this morning and, as he is chief of the tropical disease work in this territory, we were in good shape to have Osa given all possible care. She was by no means critically ill, but we were all anxious about her, particularly so in case she had the amoebic form.

Microscopic examinations were made right away and turned out all right. She had a comfortable night, and we hope that by staying over today she will be able to go on tomorrow. In the meantime, Al and I motored over the border to Aba to see what we could do to replace our three servants and two gunbearers. The manager of the transport line said he thought he could fix us out when we come along tomorrow or arrange for getting them at the next station. So you can see that at the present writing we are more or less up in the air. All we can do is to "carry on," as the English put it, and hope for the best.

We were amazingly fortunate to get the use of the district doctor's house. The porch is about nine feet wide and sixty feet long and returns around the end of the house. It has a high thatched roof, and there is plenty of room to set up the Johnsons' outfit at one end and Al's and mine at the other. The balustrade is more than a foot wide and makes a table to set things on all around, being fully protected by the overhanging thatch. We set up our table right at the entrance, and back of that is an inside dining room, and back of that a rear porch. Then across the yard from that is the kitchen, all of which we can use, as the doctor is a bachelor and has nobody around.

Yei, being on the border, is quite an important medical station, and Al has had much to interest himself in here. There is a small hospital for general cases, a group of huts for convalescent sleeping sickness patients (very few new cases), and, farther away, another group for leprosy, yaws, and a number of diseases new to me. All this sounds rather menacing for travelers, but the doctor in charge says very few white people are ever affected.

Arua, *Sunday, January* 29. The one-day layover at Yei benefited Osa so much that we decided to try and make Ferandje the next day, so we got up at daylight and were off before eight-thirty and at Aba about ten.

After the Congo customs formalities, involving a deposit on our guns, we went up to the transport station office to see about replacing our boys, who had had to leave us at Yei. The only ones they had been able to find were two convicts in jail for trouble about their wives. After looking them over, we decided to take them on. Of course the boys were glad to get out of jail.

While the negotiations were going on, Osa went over to the Mataxas house nearby to rest. Mr. Mataxas is a Greek who is majority owner of the Société du Haut Uélé et du Nil, which controls all the transportation business between Rejaf and the Congo and Uganda, and whose headquarters are at Aba. They have quite a big establish-

18. Medical Examination. Kaiser and Eastman
were interested in public health, Kaiser as a professional and Eastman
as a philanthropist. Note the spine pad worn by Eastman – protection,
it was thought, from the African sun.
(*Martin Johnson photo.*)

ment—garages, storehouses, repair shops, and so on—all built of brick made on the premises.

Mr. Mataxas is a bachelor, and his house is managed by the wife of his general manager, Mr. Constantinides. It is a large brick building with a tile-floored porch about twelve feet wide running all around it. After our business was finished, we went over there to luncheon and spent a couple of hours very pleasantly. I told them the only thing they needed to make their establishment perfect was a General Electric refrigerator. They became much interested and said they would make a special trip to Rejaf while we were gone to see the machine on the *Dal.*

We left Aba right after lunch and after a rather hot ride arrived at Ferandje about four-thirty. The district commissioner, Baron Von Zeeglen, was expecting us and had arranged for us to put up at a government rest house just across the tennis court from his own house. After taking a bath and changing our clothes, we went over to tea and met his wife, who is a very pleasant American woman. They have three children, the oldest of whom is only five or six years old. The children look very healthy, but Madame Von Zeeglen looked rather anaemic. Dr. Kaiser told her about the liver treatment, of which she had never heard. They invited us over to dinner. The baroness went over to our rest house to call on Osa, who had gone to bed on arrival as a matter of precaution, and sent some milk and fresh eggs over to Osa. The baron insisted on our coming over to breakfast with him at seven o'clock, so as to give us an early start, so we all, including Osa, went over without much demur.

The ride from Ferandje to Arua was pretty hot, and in places the discomfort was increased by having to pass through fires burning on both sides of the road. The smoke was not exactly stifling but decidedly disagreeable.

Every foot of roadway between Rejaf and Arua, which is the present end of it, is first-class gravel without ruts or bumps. We ran most of the time between fifty and sixty-five kilometers per hour. The cars are seven-passenger touring cars of Italian make, and the head driver is an Italian who speaks some English. The other three drivers are natives. It would be possible to go on up to Nairobi, but

19. Avanti! Osa Johnson stands by one of the Italian cars,
here apparently driven by the Italian professional driver, "Ed".
(*George Eastman photo.*)

some of the roads are very rough and in wet weather impassable. This is, of course, the dry season.

Phil met us on our arrival at the rest house he had reserved for us. It is a mud house, whitewashed inside and out, with thatched roof and dirt floors—one big room in each front corner, facing west, with a recessed porch in the center (much like Oak Lodge, only the roof extends out over and beyond the porch). In the rear are storerooms, and out in the rear yard are huts for the boys and one for a kitchen. (By the way, Phil has managed to collect a very fair outfit of boys, of whom he brought five from Nairobi.) Al has a tent in the front yard, and Phil sleeps in the garage, which is a kind of lean-to facing one end of the front yard. The Johnsons have the other front room like mine.

Today is Sunday, and we are lying around gossiping and making plans for the hunt. Tomorrow we shall get our licenses, which will include one for me to shoot a white rhino, which the game warden told Phil is the last one the governor will sign. If that is so, there is now no place anywhere that a permit to shoot a white rhino can be obtained, as the Congo and the Sudan have both stopped issuing licenses. Phil says the chance of my getting one is fairly good at our next camp, about thirty-five miles from here, where we shall move tomorrow afternoon.

This is a most attractive spot, on the edge of the country club, and our porch looks out for eight or ten miles across the country, the edge of which was lighted by burning grass fires last evening. The moon is just under half full and everything looks good, but it does not seem reasonable to go only thirty-five miles to shoot white rhino and only a few miles more to shoot elephant. I can't say that I am very optimistic about getting either, but I hope Al will get some antelope of different kinds, and possibly an elephant, because he can stand the walking better than I can. In view of my old-age feebleness, Phil has had a frame made out of palm stems to carry a chair in which I can sit part of the time. It will be carried by four natives. If we come up with an elephant, I suppose I may have to stand up to shoot.

Osa feels pretty well today and has spent the morning making raised bread. The rolls at luncheon were a great treat, because we have had no good bread since Khartoum, except at the meals at

Mataxas' and Baroness Von Zeeglen's. We have plenty of my gem and muffin mixtures, but sometimes it is not convenient to stop and cook them.

We have been traveling as steadily as possible for about seven weeks and are now practically as far from home as we shall get. If things go well, we shall be turning our faces homeward inside of two weeks. I am happy to say that never yet have I been sorry to do that.

There will be no chance to send more pictures until we get back to Cairo.

Yours,
G E

20. Rest Camp. The government rest houses were not elegant,
but they were clean and they greatly lessened the problems of traveling.
(*Martin Johnson photo.*)

February 3, 1928

Dear Mrs. Hutchison,

We spent Sunday the twenty-ninth at Arua arranging our outfit, and Monday morning we went to the district commissioner's office to get our Uganda licenses. Al and I procured full licenses, and Osa, who has about all the trophies, procured a bird license so she could keep in practice with her guns and help out the camp in bird food. We found that the governor had signed my special license for a white rhino, and Phil was informed that it was the last special license that would be issued. If so, the white rhino will no longer be procurable by sportsmen, as the only other places they can be found (the Congo and the Sudan) have been closed for some time. I know I tried hard to procure one in the Congo without success. Dan Pomeroy had a good deal to do with getting mine, in conjunction with his friend in the State Department.

We had lunch at our rest camp and got everything loaded up about 4:00 P.M., including about one ton of rice for our boys, which Phil had brought from Nairobi. It seems that there is a virtual famine here in Uganda, and at the last moment he was informed that he could not bring his five boys with him unless he brought their food for the whole trip. By great persistence, he succeeded in getting the twenty bags through by passenger train and boat—an almost unheard-of feat.

We arrived at this rest camp (Bullakatoni) at five-thirty, in good time to make camp. The compound is about three hundred feet front and six hundred feet deep, with a hedge all around. The ground is flat and is kept swept clean. There are three houses with straw roofs, one in the center with a porch, which I occupy. Phil and Al occupy one and Martin and Osa the other of the side houses. In the rear are seven round, thatched huts for the boys. The houses are used by the district commissioner when he holds court but can be used at all other times

21. Eastman Pasha. Amused by the
improvised sedan chair, Eastman wrote humorously that he supposed he
"may have to stand up to shoot."
(*Martin Johnson photo.*)

by travelers. The houses are whitewashed, and the dirt floors are kept swept clean, and everything is all right except for the dust raised when the wind blows. It is fourteen miles from the Nile, and we are making it our headquarters because at the rest house on the Nile the mosquitoes are very bad at night.

The next morning right after breakfast we motored down to White Rhino Camp and sat around a couple of hours, waiting for reports from the native scouts Phil had sent out, but there was nothing doing, so we ate lunch and came back. On the way down, we saw a rhino in the distance but did not like to go after him without Phil, who had motored down ahead of us to put out his scouts.

In the late afternoon, we went out to see if we could get some meat, and I shot a Uganda cob cow. On the way home, we unexpectedly came in sight of a buffalo, which Al succeeded in killing with Osa's Springfield. I was very glad he could get this rather unexpected trophy.

The next day, we followed about the same plan and ourselves picked up a rhino about half a mile from the road and stalked him for two miles, when he got our wind and made off into the bush where we could not follow him. On the way home I got one oribi for meat and a good specimen bushbuck.

The next morning, we got up before daylight and took our breakfast outfit and our two cars and one truck down to the White Rhino Camp and waited for reports from the trackers. At nine-forty-five, one came in and reported a good rhino about three miles away, so we started out afoot. I walked very easily for half an hour and then let the boys carry me in the chair for half an hour. Then I walked for a quarter of an hour and then got into the chair for another quarter of an hour. By that time (eleven-fifteen), we had arrived at the spot where our guide had left his companions to watch the rhino. Nobody was in sight, and, after sitting under a tree for half an hour while our boys searched, Phil decided that the rhino must have been disturbed and had gone away so far that the boys had got discouraged and had gone off home, for it was now three and a half hours since they had been left, so we decided to wend our way back by another route.

We were all of course disappointed and a little disheartened and thought another day of our very short visit was gone without result, but within half an hour, Phil, who was walking just ahead of my chair, threw up his hand and motioned me to get down, so my four boys let me down on the ground. I grabbed my .470 from my gunbearer and hastened after Phil, who was pointed toward a huge gray-brown object in the bushes ahead. It was our much-coveted prize—if I could get him.

He was too far away for a safe shot, so I crept up behind a bush twenty yards nearer. Even then it looked risky to me, but there was no other cover, and as the big fellow seemed to be getting suspicious and was turning I rested my gun on my forked stick and let him have it in the left fore shoulder. It was much to my surprise, I will confess, that he dropped in his tracks. We ran toward him, and as we got close we saw he was twitching, so at Phil's suggestion I gave him another shot, but he did not need it. He was an enormous brute, nearly twice as big as a black rhino, with very thick but not very long horns and a wide jaw, which distinguishes the white from the black rhinos (which are in fact nearly the same color).

We left the skinners at work and made our way back to our starting point, where the car and truck were waiting. We took the car and found Osa and Martin waiting lunch for us at three o'clock. Of course everybody was much elated at our getting the chief object of our journey, and we had a celebration at dinner with champagne and one of Eliza's suet puddings with foaming sauce.

This morning, Phil and Al and I went down to Rhino Camp to pay off the trackers, and on the way back Al got a very nice specimen Uganda cob. The Johnsons went out photographing and have just returned at twelve-thirty, having made some very good pictures of a big bull rhino that appeared to be the brother of the one I shot. Except for the heat, which is not really quite as bad as it has the reputation of being, this is ideal hunting country—rolling contour, trees and bushes enough for easy stalking, grass only waist high, no insects (except at night down on the river by White Rhino Camp, which we can avoid by sleeping here).

22. The White Rhino. This, Eastman believed,
would be the last of its kind to be shot (legally) in Africa.
The European behind Eastman is probably the Italian driver.
(*George Eastman photo.*)

The last time Phil was here, eight months ago, the lions made such a rumpus at night they had to keep fires lit all night, but just now there are none around, and Al has not had the experience yet of hearing them roar. A bull cow and calf elephant raided a nearby native shamba last night, and Phil has sent out some trackers to look for them. Martin and Osa also saw two small herds this morning, but no ivory.

In fact, the only chance we have got for elephant is down the river, where we are going on the boat, leaving White Rhino Camp at midnight tonight. We shall have to stay down there a week, whether we get anything or not. It is in the sleeping sickness district and we had to get special permission to take our boys with us. Our truck outfit will stay in camp here until we return at the end of one or two weeks—if we manage to stick it out.

Yours truly,
G E

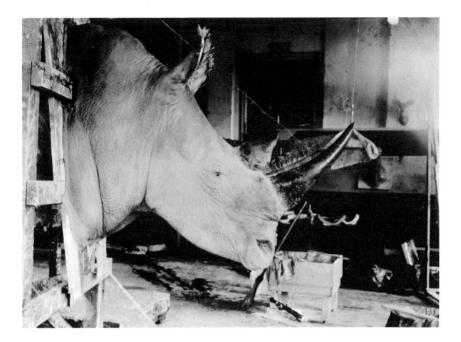

23. The White Rhino at the Taxidermist's. Mounted, the head hung
for some time in Eastman's collection. It has since disappeared.
(*Photographer unidentified. Collection of George Eastman House.*)

24. A Screened Dining Room. The whites ate in this at night,
at least once by moonlight, safe from insects.
(*Martin Johnson photo.*)

February 6, 1928

Larobi Rest Camp

Dear Mrs. Hutchison,

Al went out and shot a Uganda cob Friday morning, the day we took the steamer *Lugard* at Rhino Camp about 6:00 P.M. Just as we got to the steamer, we had another quite smart shower, but hardly more than enough to lay the dust. We left the motor outfit at our rest camp at Bullakatoni to await our return.

Phil got off the steamer the next morning at four o'clock with all our men (seven or eight) and most of our equipment to make camp for us and to inquire about elephant prospects. Al and the Johnsons and I stayed on the boat to the end of its trip at Nimule and returned with it, getting back to the camp at the rest house about 9:00 P.M., where we found everything all ready for us. Phil met us at a landing on the opposite side of the river and had dinner with us on the boat while crossing to our landing.

The *Lugard* is only a little bigger than the *Dal* and was very comfortable and clean. We saw two small herds of elephant on the way back from Nimule, in one of which was a tusker of fair size. We wanted to get off and have a try at him, but the chief of navigation, who was on the boat, said that that side of the river was closed on account of the sleeping sickness territory and we could not land without a special permit, which of course we did not have. Otherwise, the boat would have stopped and waited for us.

Phil reported that he had arranged a two-day porter safari back down the Nile again to a place where some elephants had killed a man and woman native a few days back and where the natives are very anxious to have us come and shoot them up. The porters (over a hundred men) had been engaged for Monday morning, so we had a layover of one day.

Just as lunch was called, a scout came in and reported buffaloes about a mile away, so Phil and Al started out for them. I did not go, because I already have two, killed in Tanganyika. They came back in about two hours, having got their prize—a very good specimen and an unusually tough one, for he took seven Springfield soft and two .470 hard bullets to kill him. This is Al's second buffalo. Phil says he is about fed up with buffalo—but his clients don't know any better.

Late in the afternoon, while Martin and Al were out photographing the native cotton market down by the river (our rest camp is about a mile back), I went out with Phil and got a nice Uganda cob, which I needed for my collection.

We had our dinner in a large square net tent by moonlight (full moon), with the local district commissioner as guest. This morning we got up at daylight, having had a very comfortable night, and got started with about 130 porters at seven-thirty. Osa and I were carried in the chairs and everybody else walked the ten miles, stopping fifteen minutes for rest out of every hour. We arrived here at this rest camp at twelve o'clock.

It is pretty hot in the middle of the day, but it begins to get cooler at four-thirty, and during the night one needs a very thin blanket. Everybody is well and hearty, except Martin, who has a rather bad attack of lumbago. Fortunately, he can walk, and so we propose to move seven miles to another rest camp tomorrow morning—our final camp. If all goes well, the *Lugard* will pick us up near there Saturday evening, and we will go back on her to White Rhino Camp, where our motors will be waiting for us.

These rest camps are a great boon, as they relieve us of the necessity of setting up our tents and are much more comfortable, especially in the middle of the day. They are kept swept clean and furnished with wood by the natives working for the government.

This is all sleeping sickness area around here and we had to get permits to bring Phil's servants in, but the white people don't seem to be very much afraid of it. Neither here nor in the Congo do they have it in hand among the natives the way they do in the Sudan. There, they make them live on the main road where they can inspect them and cull out the affected so they can treat them in hospital—as, for instance, Yei, which I mentioned in a previous letter.

There is nothing here but the rest camp, some native huts, and a few sheds used by the cotton buyers. There is quite a lot of cotton grown along this part of the Nile, and just now it is being brought to the steamer landings for sale to the white and East Indian traders, who ship it for ginning to White Rhino Camp, where it is baled and again shipped up through Kenya to Mombassa.

Dufile Rest Camp, *February* 8. We started for this place at 6:45 A.M. and arrived here at 9:15. I rode all the way in my chair, but Osa walked about half the seven miles. It was very comfortable, and we got here before the heat of the day.

This is our last camp, and we have five days to get our elephants. It is our last and only chance. We went out at 4:00 P.M. to look at a small herd reported by local scouts and found them at 5:00. It was an interesting stalk, but there was no tusker over thirty pounds, so without disturbing them we came back to the rest house. Phil says there are plenty of elephant around here. But to find a tusker where we can get him without too many cows around him is the problem.

We idled around camp all the next day, hoping for reports from our scouts, who are local natives directed by their headman, but nothing happened. To lose one of our remaining four hunting days was discouraging, but nothing could be done to prevent it.

Barring the heat in the middle of the day, which runs above a hundred, this is a beautiful camp. We are situated about a mile and a half from the Nile on a rise of ground that enables us to look out over a great bend in the river, which we can see in several places where the trees do not cover the view entirely. The great plain in front of us is dotted with mimosa and acacia trees and tall palms bearing great clusters of fruit shaped like oblate apples of a light orange color, of which the elephants are fond and which they get by jarring the stems of the trees, which are about eighteen inches to two feet in diameter at the base and fifty to seventy-five feet high. Back of us, the ground rises into the hills or low mountains. The distance is usually hazy, owing to the smoke from grass fires, which are usually burning somewhere along the horizon.

We are getting along very well for food, although the heat prevents our keeping any meat long enough to condition it. For instance, some chickens killed day before yesterday were spoiled yesterday when we wanted to cook them. The best way to do is to make soup and curries of the meat, or hamburger steak.

My gem mixtures come in very handy, but it is too hot to roll out the pastry. Osa made a raisin pie, using canned beef suet for the shortening; it was pretty good, although the crust was not as flaky as it ought to be. There are maggots in the flour, but we have a sieve that enables us to get rid of them. My mixtures, having been sterilized in the cans at Kodak Park, have kept perfectly.

The eggs we get from the natives (the chickens are all bantam size) are very unreliable. We can use egg powder for all the cooking, but when it comes to making the foaming sauce for one of Eliza's suet puddings, we have to rake up two fresh eggs. When we invited the assistant district commissioner to dinner the other night, we asked him to bring along two nice ones. After dinner, when I asked him if he regretted his eggs, he smacked his lips and said he would be happy to furnish two more at any time.

The water is dirty and unattractive even when boiled, so we don't drink it as a rule. We have a good supply of bottled Evian water. In fact, that is what accounts for our having to have so many porters —about fifteen of them carried chop boxes packed with Evian.

We have been very agreeably surprised at our freedom from tsetse flies and mosquitoes and other insect pests. We dine under our ten-foot-square net, because the lanterns hung outside at the corners attract a certain number of insects, but we could do without it if necessary. There are of course ants everywhere, but they do not seem to do any harm if care is taken to move all the canvas packages every day. Altogether, life in camp is not unbearable.

Personally, I never felt better in my life. Phil says he doesn't know of any other man seventy-four years old who has been out here twice to shoot elephant. In fact, he intimated that most of them know better.

25 and 26. Foot Safari. After White Rhino Camp,
the party moved south along the river, then inland on foot
to look for elephant. A hundred porters were needed. Such safaris were
sometimes strung out over a mile of trail.
(*Martin Johnson photos.*)

Friday, February 10. Yesterday we got up at daylight and by previous arrangement started out at seven o'clock for a rendezvous on the road leading along the Nile about half a mile away from the river. It was about a mile to the road and then about two miles to a magnificent spreading wild fig tree with a trunk about four feet in diameter. Here we arranged our chairs and sat down to await advice from our scouts. After about half an hour, one came in and reported a big tusker quite nearby, so we set out to come up with him—me in my chair, of course, like some Indian potentate with an umbrella.

After about half an hour, we came in sight of a bunch of two cows and the big tusker. Phil went on ahead with the glasses to look him over, and I followed on foot, of course with my gunbearer. We were about 150 yards away, and the elephants were standing dozing under a tree in full sight across a shallow donga. The big elephant looked magnificent to me. He was standing sidewise to us and his right tusk showed up in great shape, but there was a note of disappointment in Phil's voice as he said, looking at him through the glasses, "Isn't it a shame—only one perfect tusk; his left is broken off."

Phil at first was for leaving him, but when I reflected that there could be only two days more of hunting, that I might in the end not get another chance at so large a one, or in fact any at all, and that Al might not get one if I used any of the remaining time, I decided we ought to take him.

So Phil and my gunbearer and I began to stalk the bunch. They were in an ideal position and the wind was right. We got across the donga, and I was just getting my gun in position when the bull turned and started to walk away. I asked Phil if I should take the rump shot, and on his saying yes I fired; then he fired, and we both hit him and raked him fore and aft with our .470s.

The cows disappeared in a flash, which relieved us of that worry, and the bull went slowly on. We followed him up, and I had to put five more of the big bullets in him before he went down. Martin was close behind us using his Eyemo; and Osa, working the tripod motion picture camera, and Al the Cine Kodak, were across the donga doing their best to photograph the scene.

27. Waiting for Elephant. Surely one of the most
beautiful photographs Martin Johnson ever took – the long wait under the
giant fig tree. Eastman is almost certainly under the umbrella.
(*Martin Johnson photo.*)

28. Elephant. With this kill,
Eastman completed his African quest. He was seventy-four.
(*George Eastman photo.*)

When we got close to the big fellow and I realized what a magnificent brute he was, I was glad I had made the decision to take him. His missing tusk can be replaced by the taxidermist, and the fact that it was missing when I killed him has no significance, except to a pot hunter shooting for the value of the ivory.

After having some closeups made, we went back to our tree for lunch and to wait for the skinners, who had been sent for, leaving two of our boys to guard the booty. It was only about ten o'clock, and it would take two hours for the messenger and their return. After lunch we decided to stay under our tree until the sun moderated a little. I sat reading one of Phil's books in the shade when my arm began to burn. My sleeve was rolled up, but it never occurred to me that I could get sunburned in the shade of a tree; but when I looked down, my forearms were as red as beets from the stray rays that filtered through the foliage. Of course, I had my sun hat on and my face was more protected, but even that was burning a little, too, from the reflected rays from the sand.

At four o'clock, we left Phil, who thought he ought to go back and see how the skinners were getting along, and made our way back to camp, which we reached in about an hour. Phil did not return until nearly seven-thirty, quite after dark, when he came in alone, his gunbearer having stopped to get some of the blood off his hands after helping at the carcass. Phil said the walk along that road and the last half hour cross-country to the camp without a gun had got on his nerves. He had had to go into a native village and get a couple of men to show him the way to camp in the dark.

He gave a graphic account of the scene at the carcass. All the afternoon, groups of natives were passing our tree on the way to the scene of the killing. By the time he got there just before sundown, there must have been more than two hundred natives, from small boys not more than six or seven years old to women carrying their babies (in a sling I shall later describe) and men with knives ready for the butchering. The chief was there and had the situation well in hand, but it was difficult. Our skinners would not let anybody touch the carcass until they had skinned the head, cut off the tail and two feet, and chopped out the tusks, which were the parts to be saved. In order to skin the head, they had to roll the carcass over. It was so heavy (Phil estimated five tons) that all of the crowd who could get hold of it could not budge it, so the skinners decided to disembowel it. Before this, the crowd had got so impatient that the chief or headman had taken all their knives away to prevent casualties among the fighters. (It must be remembered that this is a famine time in this country, and most of the inhabitants are actually suffering for food, and the prospect of a supply set them fairly crazy to get at it.)

As soon as the intestines were out and the carcass was turned over, the crowd burst loose and running for their knives began hacking for meat, the men with knives throwing pieces to members of their families in the outer line. Phil said it was pandemonium broken loose. It must have been a vivid scene, lighted by brush-wood fires as the light went out of the sky.

The two skinners worked hard and told Phil they hoped to get their part of the carcass down to the road last night. Phil estimates that it would take at least thirty porters to carry the load mentioned— the head skin, including the trunk; two legs; the tail; and two feet (without the skull)—before thinning weighing probably over a thousand pounds. It will take them all day to pare down the skin from the inside so the salt will soak in far enough to preserve it. They had to give it a bath of salt outside and inside as they went along with the skinning. In fact, there is great difficulty in preparing any such large skin so it will not spoil in this weather.

We had a fine dinner. Osa had the cook make a mutton stew, and she made the dumplings out of my biscuit mixture. She also made a rice pudding using dried egg. And I showed her how to make hard sauce, which, strange to say, was new to her. We used Bombay canned butter, which is the only grease except beef drippings that does not melt in this temperature. It is not rancid, but of course it has not the flavor of fresh butter. You may be sure we loaded up the sauce with plenty of the sherry that we brought along for the foaming sauce. Altogether, the rice pudding was a success.

Al went out with Phil at seven this morning to try and get his elephant. Martin went with them to photograph. They thought they might be back to lunch, but it is now after three and they have not

29. The Tusk. Almost as tall as the man who took it,
the tusk weighed sixty-four pounds.
(*Martin Johnson photo.*)

turned up, so I am hoping they have found something. Osa went out this morning with the .22 and came back with four guinea hens as fat as butter. She is having them prepared for dinner.

Tomorrow will be the last day of elephant hunting, for there is mighty little chance of getting one going down the Nile on the *Dal*. We are all hoping Al will get one; he is such a good sport in every way. The *Lugard* will stop and pick us up about five tomorrow evening and this will be posted on the boat.

Ever yours,

G E

30. The Elephant at the Taxidermist's.
"Fitting the ears – Jonas Brothers" is the pencilled caption on this print.
(*Photographer unidentified. Collection of George Eastman House.*)

31. At Eastman House. The elephant had come to rest
in the place where Eastman had intended, its missing tusk
replaced by one of wood. The mounted head has since decomposed.
(*Photographer unidentified. Collection of George Eastman House.*)

Monday, February 20, 1928

Dear Mrs. Hutchison,

We found Ed waiting with the cars and trucks at the landing at White Rhino Camp when the *Lugard* came to the landing at seven o'clock Sunday morning, the twelfth. We had breakfasted on the boat and we set out for Arua as soon as we could load our equipment. We stopped at the rest camp at Bullakatoni to get our white rhino trophies and arrived at Arua by ten o'clock. We spent the day at the rest house where we had stopped before and prepared for as early a getaway for the long run to Aba as our necessary formalities with the game authorities would permit. In order to give notice to Mr. Metaxas that we were going to accept his invitation to stay overnight at his house, we loaded up one of the trucks and started it off the evening before.

We were up at daylight Monday morning, but it took us until half past nine to get through all the formalities, including the weighing and stamping of the tusk (which proved to be sixty-four pounds. It is seventy-seven and a half inches long, measured on the curve, and when it stands on the ground it is higher than my head. It is a good, husky piece of ivory and is seventeen and a half inches in circumference at the base. In order to hang the head where I want to, over the door in the music room leading to the terrace, I shall have it set up with false tusks to save weight, and stand the one tusk on the floor.) This is a digression. To resume: we reached Aba about 6:30 P.M., had a nice dinner, a good sleep and breakfast, and started for Rejaf at nine-thirty, arriving there at six-thirty after a blistering hot ride over a mostly desert country. We had baths and cold drinks and soon felt comfortable.

The next day the Johnsons spent in arranging their start for Nairobi, intending to visit the Elephant Farm, the pygmies, and some points of photographic interest on Lake Albert en route. I gave them my cots and air beds, chairs, chop-boxes, one of my Mannlichers with hard bullets, and a supply of food to last them a couple of weeks. They took one of the trucks we had been using.

That evening, Osa and I went over to the district commissioner's, Mr. Burgess's, and had a cocktail made with ice off the *Dal*, and afterward Al and Phil and I went over to his bungalow to dinner. Osa stayed with Martin, who was feeling a little poorly. Perhaps they were fortunate, because something at the dinner—Al thinks it was the fish course—upset Al and me so much that the next day we were confined to the boat. Phil escaped because he did not take the fish. However, we had a very pleasant evening, listening to the phonograph out under the stars after dinner. We took over Osa's record of the "Two Black Crows," which was new to Burgess. Also a couple of bottles of Pommery Sec right off the ice.

Burgess was enthusiastic about the daily supply of ice he had from the *Dal* during the two weeks we were away. He had some thermos bottles, into which he put it, and it kept him in cool drinks all the time.

We had left at Aba my convict tent boy, whom I had taken out of jail to go on the Arua trip. He proved to be the best one of all we had with us, quick to learn and unusually intelligent for a native. I was sorry to part with him and tried to get the authorities at Aba to lighten his sentence.

You never can tell what trouble with women will lead to. They told a story about a boy who was up for baptism at the mission, but the missionary refused to baptize him because he had three wives, so he went off disconsolate. In a few days he came back all smiles. "You baptize me now—only have one wife," he said. The missionary asked him what he had done with the other two, and he replied, "Me kill 'em."

We had a lot of trouble at Rejaf to get our trophies through the customs so we could take them with us to Khartoum. The man in charge was a native, who, while anxious to please, was very technical and insisted on our sending them by mail steamer. It was only after wiring to the head authorities at Khartoum that we got permission to bring them on our boat. They were not fully cured and needed atten-

32. Martin and Osa Johnson. The Johnsons and Eastman
parted at Rejaf; they were not to see each other again.
(*Martin Johnson photo.*)

tion to keep them from spoiling. Wouldn't it have been tragic to lose them after all our trouble?

Friday after breakfast we pulled out from the dock, headed north for Khartoum, leaving the Johnsons standing disconsolate on the dock, Martin cranking his movie and Osa in tears. We were all feeling very sad, for they had been excellent company. Osa lent us her Springfield (by mistake her ammunition had been sent all soft-nose and was no good for dangerous game). Phil will take it to her at Nairobi via Port Sudan. As I said before, I had given her one of my Mannlichers with hard-nose cartridges.

It is very comfortable to be back on the *Dal*, where we can have plenty of clean linen, cool drinks, and good food (excepting yeast bread). The cook makes bread that is not fit even for toast. His yeast seems to be at fault. I have been told that dry yeast cakes won't keep in this climate, but if I were to come again I would certainly try them, bedding them in my bread mixture after sterilization and cooling of the flour.

Some of the flour they have on the boat has maggots in it, but they do no great harm, as they can be sifted out. They are nice clean-looking little things, anyway. I remember that on one of my western trips, before I got posted on sterilization, the maggots got into the flour and I had no sieve. You can bet I never mentioned the situation to the other members of the party. I picked out all I *saw* and let it go at that.

The day after leaving Rejaf, we began to see elephants, but no large ivory. The second day (Sunday), however, some were seen about a mile away, one of which looked promising, so Al and Phil started off with my .470s and the gunbearers. They soon disappeared in the grass. About an hour after, a boy came hurrying back with the message that Al had got his elephant and wanted his Cine Kodak. After another hour, Al and Phil and three gunbearers appeared. All were wet to the waist but were very happy because they had been successful.

It seems this particular bunch of elephants when first seen were in short grass but on the edge of a swamp, into which they had strayed before the hunters got up with them. To get close enough to shoot, they had to wade up to their hips, and in one place both had to be carried on the shoulders of the askaris; and in another, Al, who is short, had to actually swim a couple of yards. However, they finally got where Al could get a shot at the bull, and he brought him to his knees with two shots in quick succession. Then the cows began to trumpet. The elephant got on his feet, and Al had to floor him again. Then Al began to shoot over the heads of the cows to drive them away. The angle was too much for him, and the heavy gun kicked him over backward into the water. The cows disappeared at this juncture, fortunately, and all was well.

The boys were left to chop out the tusks and cut off the feet and tail, and the hunters came back to the boat. Almost as if by wireless, the news spread to some native villages nearby, and men, women, and children began to wend their way to the booty that they knew would be theirs.

Thus ends another chapter in our story. We have now got the major things we came after, without mishap. We have an extra week in which to get hippos and Nile perch and a few antelope we need for our collections, so we can leisurely make our way down the river to Khartoum in a satisfied frame of mind.

Friday, February 24. Sunday night (the day Al got his elephant), we received a wire from Harper Sibley when we reached Bor saying that he and Streeter hoped to see us at Rejaf. Unfortunately, we had passed him somewhere on the river, so I had to wire him our regrets.

That night, we tied up at Shambe, the headquarters of the Neuer war, and got all the news from the Syrian doctor. It seems the natives were driven into the swamp with their cattle and bombed from the ten planes. Forty or fifty natives and several thousand cattle were killed and three ringleaders captured, one escaping. The man who actually killed Ferguson tried to escape and they had to kill him, much to their regret, as they wanted to execute him with some ceremony. The fourth is still at large, but they expect to get him. In the meantime, the whole tribe became terrified, and men, women, and children scrambled for headquarters, begging for mercy. This was what the authorities were after, and they probably won't kill any

33 and 34. Kaiser's Elephant Hunt.
It was wet along the Nile, and Percival and Kaiser both got a ducking –
but he got his elephant.
(*George Eastman photos.*)

more of them until they see how they behave after this scare. They are, however, a thorough bad lot and may have to be wiped out before the district can be cleared up.

The next day, as on several days, we saw lots of elephant but no good ivory. Early Tuesday morning, we saw on the bank some lechwe, rare antelope with horns something like the Kenya impalla's, and so we tied up and went after them. I went in one direction with Phil and my gunbearer, and Al and his gunbearer went in the other. We had not gone over 500 yards before my boy excitedly handed me my gun and pointed through the bushes. I did not get my eyes on the animal for several seconds; then, as I was taking aim, he broke away into the bushes. I had a full view of him for just an instant, and it made me just sick to lose such a magnificent animal, but there was no help for it, and we went on through broken reeds and some bush. Presently Phil, who was behind me, gave a low whistle. This time I was quicker, but the animal was quicker still and was bounding away when I fired. I could hear the bullet strike, but he did not go down.

Then began the prettiest piece of stalking it has been my privilege to see. The gunbearer made his way to the point where the animal had disappeared in the high grass and soon picked up some bloodstained blades of grass. From there on, he followed him by the very occasional blood smears through the high, dead grass, twisting in and out of paths broken by previous animals. Once, we caught sight of him and I fired but missed. Soon, we had no bloodstains to guide us, but on the tracker went. I was sure we had lost the animal, particularly because he changed direction and went toward where Al had disappeared. After a little while, we met Al and his bearer coming our way. Al had got one shot at another buck but had missed him, as the buck was running too fast.

I was all in by this time and started back to the boat, leaving the finish to Phil and the tracker. After a little while, the buck was found lying in the grass, but when Phil fired at him he got up and made a new start; however, they got him soon, as he could not run very far.

Phil complimented me on my first shot, particularly as it was made with the telescope sight, which he has not got used to. I like it better than an open sight, even on moving objects.

[73]

That night we anchored in Lake No, and in the morning we had some good fishing for Nile Perch and tigerfish. The perch run to seventy-five or a hundred pounds, but we got nothing over five or six pounds. They are sassy strikers and fighters, and we had some good sport. The tigerfish is an ugly-looking devil with sharp teeth projecting from his mouth.

We left Lake No at 11:00 A.M. for a side trip up the Bahr el Ghazal to get white-eared cob. On the way, we saw a small bunch of lechwe, and Al and my bearer went ashore and Al got a specimen. This was great luck, as they are quite rare, as I said before. This morning we got up at daybreak and got out on the veldt by six-thirty. Before ten-thirty, each of us had got two specimens of the white-eared cob, which we needed to compare with our Uganda cobs, which have red ears. We are now on our way back to Lake No, having had a delightful little side trip—no insects and quite comfortable temperature, as it was cloudy all the morning.

Sunday, February 26. We stopped at Lake No overnight. Al and Phil fished in the late afternoon, getting some tigerfish and Nile perch, but nothing notable. I went out for an hour after breakfast and succeeded in landing a fair-sized perch weighing forty or fifty pounds and measuring forty inches long. He was quite sporty, but my tackle was too heavy to give him much of a chance to show what he could do.

We got to Mongalla late in the evening and tied up at the dock to wait for the mail boat, which was a day overdue. We received by her a few letters, among mine a lot of clippings and a letter from Dr. Burkhart bringing news of the happenings in Rochester, up to and including the organization of the new council, the favorable report by the committee on having the civic center on the river at Broad Street, and a letter from you announcing you propose sailing with Charles from San Francisco on Washington's Birthday on a trip around the world via Australia, which pleased me very much. I hope we shall meet on the Continent or in London.

35. Nile Perch. Product of an hour's after-breakfast fishing.
(*George Eastman photo.*)

Khartoum, *March* 6. The rest of the journey down the Nile was uneventful and uninteresting. We were held up above the bridge at Rink for nearly twenty-four hours on account of low water and a confusion of orders, so we did not get to Khartoum until noon. Here we heard that the bridge would not open until daylight this morning, but they finally transferred us to our barge and with a tug took us *under* the bridge. We were at the hotel by two-thirty. Here we found a lot of mail, which busied us until the barber shop opened at 4:00 P.M. My hair, not having been cut for two months, was almost long enough to braid. A hot bath in clear, white water was most refreshing. We found that the hour for leaving for Luxor had been changed from evening to morning on account of low water and that consequently our stay would be only two nights and one full day; hence, it will be a rush job to get our trophies crated and shipped.

Phil is disappointed not to find a boat out of Port Sudan for nearly three weeks, and he may go back up the Nile on the *Dal* and home that way and save about two weeks. He met Mr. Rothschild in Nairobi and got an invitation to go that way.

I did not find much personal mail here. I suppose it is in Cairo. We shall spend two days in Luxor and reach Cairo March thirteenth and sail for Messina or Naples on the *Adriatic* the twenty-fifth. Al and I expect to make a little trip in southern Italy before he leaves me.

The big trip is now over, and this will be my last general letter. All the rest will be regular tourist stuff, and the description of it is out of my line.

I hope to be home by the middle of June, in time for the strawberries and raspberries.

Yours,
Geo Eastman

36. Down the Nile. The return was "uneventful and uninteresting,"
but there were many of the same things to see as on the trip south.
(*Martin Johnson photo.*)

NOTES

Page xvii. *His first hunting safari.* Eastman; Akeley; Johnson, 1940.

Page xviii. *firm arrangements for a second trip.* Butterfield PLB23. Cable, Eastman to Mrs. Philip Percival, 23 March 1927.

Page xviii. *"no white rhino can now be found."* Arlott and Williams, p. 154.

Page xviii. *Leasing a steamer.* Butterfield PLB23, Eastman to F.C. Mattison, 9 May 1927.

Page xviii. *Gordon . . . steamers.* Moorehead, 1960, p. 183ff.

Page xix. *Albert Kaiser.* Kaiser's experiences on the trip are summarized in interviews in the Rochester *Times-Union* and *Democrat and Chronicle*, 23 April 1928.

Page xix. *model for the white hunter in* The Green Hills. Baker, p. 333.

Page xix. *Eastman's life as an outdoorsman.* Macomber.

Page xix. *camping gadgets.* The Eastman House International Museum of Photography has an album of photographs of Eastman's camping gear, some with his notes. See also Butterfield IEH, Padelford interview.

Page xix. *African Hall.* Akeley, pp. 3–4.

Page xx. *He brought good tools.* Democrat and Chronicle, 2 November 1927.

Page xx. *Osa's telescopic sight.* This sight and the rifle on which it was mounted may have stayed in Eastman's collection, for Eastman's chauffeur remembered only two Mannlichers and a Springfield, the latter with a "telescope and hairline sights," a superior rifle "elegantly finished." Butterfield IEH, Padelford interview.

Page xxi. *rifles of enormous power.* J.A. Hunter thought anything smaller than .450 "unwise" for elephant, rhino, or buffalo; calibres to .600 did not seem overlarge to him, his own favorite being .500. Hunter, pp. 220–221.

Page xxi. *suicide note.* "To my friends My work is done why wait? GE." Photographic reproduction of the note, in *The University of Rochester Library Bulletin*, XXVI, 3 (Spring, 1971), p. 123.

Page xxii. *Pommery Sec.* "4 cases of good Scotch whiskey, I leave the Brand to C. [Cook] & Son. 2 cases of Pommery Extra Sec, qts. 1 case of [Pommery Extra Sec] pts." Butterfield LEK 1927, Eastman to F.C. Mattison.

Page xxii. *enthusiasm for cooking.* Macomber, p. 91.

Page xxii. *four young married women.* Collins, p. 103: ". . . four young Rochester matrons . . . all in their early thirties . . . had lunch with Mr. Eastman regularly on Saturdays and came to have an unusually close relationship with him."

Page xxii. *Osa Johnson.* Johnson 1940, 1941. Gleason, p. 99: ". . . there was a naive simplicity about her that was childlike and lovable. . . ."

Page xxiii. *underwriting Johnson's photography.* Eastman was one of a number of underwriters. Johnson had the backing, as well, of the American Museum of Natural History and of a limited stock company.

Page xxiii. *as a modern historian has put it.* MacCarthy, p. 82.

Page xxiii. *the racism of the day.* Gleason, p. 97: "G.E.'s attitude toward Negroes was typical of his time—paternalistic, but strictly against fraternization."

Page 3. *new shop in the Place Vendôme.* Eastman seems to have visited the Kodak store in every city he passed through.

Page 3. *Royal Free Hospital.* Eastman's many philanthropies were particularly strong in education and health.

Page 3. *Dr. Burkhart.* Harvey J. Burkhart, director of the Rochester Dental Dispensary, an Eastman philanthropy.

Page 3. *Bouveng.* Nils Bouveng, a London associate.

Page 4. *Osa.* Osa Johnson.

Page 4. *Al.* Albert Kaiser, his physician on this trip.

Page 5. *francs.* There were then about twenty-five francs to the dollar.

Page 6. *"Shepheards".* Shepheards Hotel, the great old Cairo hostelry.

Page 6. *Mr. Nassibian.* The local Kodak representative?

Page 7. *the big dam.* At Assuan, considerably predating the "high dam" that led to the moving of the Abu Simbel temple.

Page 8. *the* Dal. The ship leased and refurbished for him by Cook's.

Page 10. *our licenses.* By this date, most game was licensed, and had in fact been so for many years because of hunting pressure. Large areas of Somalia and South Africa were said to have been "shot out" before hunting in British East Africa really got underway in the nineties, and this experience, coupled with the increased pressure brought by better transportation and better weapons, led to a pan-European movement for African hunting control in the late Victorian period. Nonetheless, the great game herds had been greatly reduced (not entirely by hunting). Not all animals were licensed—the lion, for example, did not go on the East African license until 1937.

Page 10. *our nice biscuit mixtures.* The plural possessive was often used by Eastman; the mixtures—dry ingredients for non-yeast breads and muffins— were a great favorite of his. He even had them sterilized at the Kodak works in Rochester.

Page 10. *Khartoum.* Capital of the Sudan, site of Gordon's defeat and death.

Page 10. *Omdurman.* Site of the British victory over indigenous forces in 1898.

Page 10. *the Mahdi.* Mohammed Ahmed, Islamic spiritual and political leader who overthrew Gordon.

Page 10. *the Kitchener battlefield.* Site of the 1898 battle.

Page 12. *the Sudan government.* Sudan was ruled under an Egyptian-British Condominium, the real authority being British.

Page 12. At end of letter 3: "Not for duplication. Dr Mrs. H. The shingles are almost gone and are giving no further trouble and I am sleeping well and getting my strength back. Hence I am expecting to enjoy the trip on the Dal to the full. GE / If there are any repetitions please cut them out."

Page 15. *the one in British East Africa.* Eastman's first African trip, described in *Chronicles of an African Trip.*

Page 16. *the natives who murdered Ferguson.* Members of the Neuer tribe.

Page 16. *Ferguson the government agent.* Captain Vele Ferguson, the District Commissioner, had only recently been killed.

Page 18. *roan antelope.* A large antelope, horned in both sexes. Williams and Arlott, p. 198.

Page 18. *Tommy.* A Thompson's gazelle. An abundant, quite small gazelle (two feet at shoulder.) Williams and Arlott, p. 197.

Page 18. *shikaris.* "Hunters" (Urdu), a term from the hunting practices of the Raj.

Page 23. An envelope is included among the pages before Letter 5. On it is written, in a hand probably not Eastman's, "Negatives with Lansing. Other negatives to Mr. Craig for Dr. Kaiser (14)."

Page 24. *a chief.* "Chief" was not a word with great African meaning, although it became a political term under British rule.

Page 24. *the Sudd*. Moorehead, 1960, calls this papyrus swamp "the great obstacle" (p. 95) and a "claustrophobic green prison" (p. 157). Samuel Baker and his wife were trapped there for months by the floating debris that regularly choked the channels. By Eastman's day, the channels had been cleared.

Page 27. *wheat gems*. Eastman's sterilized whole wheat flour.

Page 27. *Eliza's suet pudding with foaming sauce*. The following recipe is from "a cookbook with cover and title page missing," supplied by Sondra Updike Alden of the Osa and Martin Johnson Safari Museum:

Suet Pudding

1 cup ground suet	2 teaspoons baking powder
1 cup molasses	½ teaspoon salt
1 cup raisins	1 teaspoon cloves
1 cup currants	1 teaspoon cinnamon
3 cups sifted all-purpose flour	1½ cups milk

Combine suet, molasses, raisins and currants. Sift together dry ingredients; add to suet mixture alternately with milk, beating until smooth after each addition. Turn into buttered 2-quart mold, cover tightly and steam 5 hours. Serve with Lemon Sauce, Hard Sauce, or Foamy Egg Sauce.

(This is effectively my grandmother's Plum Pudding. KMC.)

Eliza's Foaming Sauce
(from Johnson, 1941, but undoubtedly Eastman's recipe because of the name Eliza)
½ cup butter
1 cup sugar
1 egg

Cream butter and sugar. Add yolk and stand over boiling water. When melted, add 1 tablespoon boiling water and 2 tablespoons sherry. When ready to serve, add beaten white of egg.

Page 27. *see picture*. The picture has not survived.

Page 28. *the donkeys and sheep*. The sheep were not mentioned in the earlier list, nor were the goats of which he wrote on January 18. Perhaps these had just been acquired. They were probably carried for food, being butchered just before cooking because of the heat.

Page 31. A separate slip of paper is included before letter 6. On it is written, in the same hand as before and probably not Eastman's, "6 negatives to Mr. Craig for Dr. Kaiser."

Page 31. *the Neuers*. This large, powerful tribe had given the British difficulties for years.

Page 31. *a witch doctor*. Two of the Neuer "witch doctors" became so famous in England that they "achieved the distinction of a verse in *Punch*" (Henderson, p. 159). Exactly what a "witch doctor" is, the term being Western and the view Christian, remains unclear.

Page 31. *Dinkas*. Eastman may not have seen a representative group: Heminway (p. 264) saw them as warriors "sometimes six and a half feet tall, herding goats," and he liked another writer's description of their composing "love songs to their cattle"—although they are not alone in Africa in doing that.

Page 32. *good ivory*. Tusks over thirty pounds each.

Page 32. *a very good waterbuck*. A handsome, big antelope with a noticeably shaggy coat; thought by some to be not only tough but also bad-tasting.

Page 34. *gave him up reluctantly*. Leaving a wounded animal, at least of the antelope type, was done more often than we care to believe. If Percival had been with him, more persistence might have been shown.

Page 34. *a tiang*. An antelope related to the topi.

Page 34. *B. E. A.* British East Africa (on the first safari).

Page 37. On a separate page before the beginning of the seventh letter is written, perhaps in Eastman's hand, "This should be #7." Eastman had written an 8 at the top of the letter and had numbered all subsequent letters accordingly. However, there is no gap in the account and it is clear that no letter is missing.

Page 42. *Phil*. Philip Percival, who had come up from Nairobi with cars, trucks, food, and men. His original plan had been to organize the entire safari from Safariland in Nairobi; however, Sudanese officials apparently insisted that local labor be used. Butterfield PLB24 nos. 116 and 118, 23 September 1927; and PLB23 no. 475, Philip Percival to Safariland, 14 July 1927.

Page 42. *Oak Lodge*. Eastman's place in North Carolina.

Page 42. *white rhino*. "After the Elephants . . . the largest of the land mammals, weighing about 3,550kg (3½ tons)." (Williams and Arlott, p. 187.) Now exceedingly rare, it is represented in Kenya by a few animals kept under armed guard because of poachers, who kill rhino (sometimes with poisoned arrows) for the horn alone. Evidently not so much ferocious as near-sighted, the Kenyan white rhinos are herded about by their guards with whacks of a rifle butt.

Page 45. *about all of the trophies*. Osa Johnson was an excellent shot and had lived in Africa for years.

Page 45. *Dan Pomeroy*. Daniel Pomery, a member of the first Eastman safari.

Page 45. *one ton of rice.* Maize meal (Kiswahili *ugali,* called in colonial days *posho,* a term no longer common) was the recognized staple of safari labor; the amount to be provided per day was controlled by law. A ton of rice for five men for two weeks is impossible; perhaps Ugandan authorities had ruled that Percival must supply rice for all of the Ugandan laborers as well as the five Kenyans (at about one pound per man per day).

Page 45. *by passenger train and boat.* It is unclear why the rice did not come by truck.

Page 47. *White Rhino Camp.* Actually a village; a camp in the old days. Mentioned by many travelers (e.g., Moorehead 1959, de Wattville) and still on the map.

Page 47. *Uganda kob.* An antelope about three feet at the shoulder, only the male horned. Williams and Arlott, p. 195.

Page 47. *oribi.* A small antelope (two feet at the shoulder), horned only in the male. Williams and Arlott, p. 194.

Page 47. *bushbuck.* A shy antelope about three feet at the shoulder, with spiral horns in the male. Williams and Arlott, p. 226.

Page 48. *my forked stick.* Did Eastman use a gun rest? This is the only mention of it.

Page 48. *nearly twice as big as a black rhino.* Not really.

Page 50. *shamba.* "Farm" (Kiswahili).

Page 50. *down the river.* Downstream on this same navigable stretch of the Nile, between Lake Albert and Nimule, where the rapids began.

Page 53. *the end of its trip.* The steamer turned around, navigation being impossible in the rapids.

Page 53. *over a hundred men.* This was a large number for such a short safari. Eastman explains one reason for needing so many on 8 February. Too, Percival would have needed many men to carry out an elephant trophy. After a certain point, of course, more porters were needed simply to carry food for the porters. Loads were limited to sixty pounds.

Page 54. *fed up with buffalo.* Many hunters considered buffalo the most dangerous game animal—unpredictable, fast, aggressive. Clients who wanted to hunt it with .30-caliber rifles—a growing fashion in the twenties—probably lowered Percival's enthusiasm. Eastman's account of the shooting—seven Springfield (.30-calibre) and two .470 bullets—suggests that Percival used the heavy double-barreled rifle after the client had peppered the buffalo with soft-nosed, small-caliber shots, although it may be that Kaiser switched guns and finished the animal with the .470 himself.

Page 55. *tusker*. Still the term for a trophy elephant.

Page 58. *shallow donga*. "Gully" (Kiswahili, but no longer common).

Page 58. *I fired; then he fired*. The trophy belonged to whoever fired first. The white hunter, of course, never fired first—even when he fired first. There is no reason to suspect Eastman's account. Percival, however, was probably quick to follow up, not wanting a wounded elephant either charging them or roaming about the countryside with his client's bullet in it. He also wanted Eastman to get his trophy, of course.

Page 58. *that worry*. The cows might have charged or got in the way of further shots or even assisted the bull.

Page 58. *Eyemo*. A movie camera.

Page 58. *Cine Kodak*. Kodak-made movie camera.

Page 61. *his missing tusk*. In the trophy-mad atmosphere of much big game hunting, particularly among those infected by Rowland Ward's annual listing of record kills, a one-tusked elephant would have been rejected. Eastman's reasoning was quite valid, however: the elephant was no less large or dangerous for having only one piece of ivory.

Page 61. *a sling I shall later describe*. He did not.

Page 61. *the parts to be saved*. Elephant heads were commonly mounted as trophies; the tails were often kept, as well, the thick black hairs made into various trinkets. Elephant feet were sometimes used to make useful items like umbrella stands.

Page 62. *a vivid scene*. The butchering of an elephant carcass is a scene often described by whites who seemed unaware how rare a thing meat was in East Africa.

Page 62. *before thinning*. The skin just after removal was thick and heavy, and fat and tissue adhered to it. In camp, the skinners removed all extraneous matter, then carefully thinned the hide itself, a job that could take days with an animal as big as an elephant. (See, for example, de Wattville, p. 237.)

Page 64. *guinea hens*. Large, abundant fowl that occur in flocks.

Page 67. *Ed*. The Italian driver?

Page 67. *sixty-four pounds*. A hundred-pound tusk was considered big; this one, as Eastman shows, was certainly big enough.

Page 67. *In order to hang the head.* The elephant head, with false tusks as he planned, was hung where he intended in the music room; a photograph shows the single real tusk standing on the floor. After Eastman's death, the head and the tusk passed through various institutional hands, and the head, forgotten in storage, became the prey of vermin and decay, and it no longer exists. The single tusk, however, remains—a mystery to its present stewards until its origins were explained. A few other heads (probably from the first safari) are said to exist in Rochester government offices. Eastman's white rhino, like most of its kind on earth, has disappeared—it, too, presumably falling prey to vermin and rot in storage.

Page 67. *the Elephant Farm.* A scheme for domesticating African elephants at Wandra, the then Belgian Congo.

Page 70. *Osa in tears.* Each saw the other as in tears: "Tears filled his kindly eyes. 'I'm going to ship you back my electric refrigerator, Osa,' he said, and disappeared into his cabin." Johnson 1940, p. 307.

Page 71. *askaris.* "Soldiers" (Kiswahili), but probably Eastman's error for "shikaris."

Page 71. *Nile perch.* A rough fish that goes to very large sizes.

Page 71. *Harper Sibley.* Of Rochester, New York.

Page 71. *Streeter.* Unidentified, unless this is Daniel Streeter of Buffalo, New York, author of *Denatured Africa* (which the white hunter of Hemingway's *Green Hills of Africa*—based on Phil Percival—called the best book about safari hunting) and of *Camels!*.

Page 71. *the Syrian doctor.* Called Armenian before.

Page 73. *lechwe.* As Eastman notes, another antelope.

Page 73. *leaving the finish.* This was one of the ways white hunters earned their money.

Page 74. *Lake No.* A small lake at the northern limit of the Sudd, formed by a Nile tributary.

Page 74. *Bahr el Ghaẓal.* A Nile tributary.

Page 74. *white-eared cob.* Another of the antelopes.

Page 76. *Mr. Rothschild.* Unidentified.

Page 76. *Luxor.* On the way from this historic site to Cairo, Eastman and Kaiser lost most of their belongings in a fire on the train, both having been roused from sleep and made to leave the train in pyjamas. "Naturally it isn't much fun to see your stuff go up in flames," Kaiser was quoted as saying later, but they were happy "to escape as well as we did without quibbling about trifles." Rochester *Democrat and Chronicle*, 23 March 1928.

BIBLIOGRAPHY

AKELEY, MARY L. JOBE. *Carl Akeley's Africa*. New York: Blue Ribbon Books, 1929.

BAKER, CARLOS. *Ernest Hemingway: a Life Story*. New York: [1969] Discus/Avon, 1980.

BUTTERFIELD, ROGER. Papers in the collection of the Libraries of the University of Rochester.

COLLINS, ROWLAND. Introduction to "Ever Yours, GE," in *The University of Rochester Library Bulletin*, XXVI, 3 (Spring, 1971).

DE WATTVILLE, VIVIENNE. *Out in the Blue*. London: Methuen and Co., 1927.

EASTMAN, GEORGE. *Chronicles of an African Trip*. Rochester, New York: privately printed, 1927.

GLEASON, MARION. "The George Eastman I Knew," in *Library Bulletin* (see Collins).

HEMINWAY, JOHN. *No Man's Land: The Last of White Africa*. New York: E.P. Dutton, 1983.

HENDERSON, K.D.D. *The Sudan Republic*. New York: Praeger, 1965.

HUNTER, J.A. *Hunter*. New York: Harper and Brothers, 1952.

JOHNSON, OSA. *I Married Adventure*. New York: Lippincott, 1940.

—— *Four Years in Paradise*. Garden City, New Jersey: Garden City Publishing Company, 1941.

MACOMBER, FRANCIS, S. "A Different Sort of World," in *Library Bulletin* (see Collins).

MCCARTHY, MICHAEL J. "Africa and America: A Study of American Attitudes Toward Africa and the Africans During the Late Nineteenth and Early Twentieth Centuries." Ph.D. diss., University of Minnesota, 1975. DDJ75–27215.

MOOREHEAD, ALAN. *No Room in the Ark*. New York: Harper and Brothers, 1959.

—— *The White Nile*. New York: [1960] Dell, 1962.

WILLIAMS, JOHN G., and NORMAN ARLOTT. *A Field Guide to the National Parks of East Africa*. London: Collins, 1981.

This book was produced under the direction of Horace Hart.
It was designed by Howard I. Gralla.
The map for the end leaves was drawn by Jeanyee Wong.
The typeface is Monotype Fournier and was set
by Michael & Winifred Bixler.
The paper is Mohawk Superfine Text.
The book was printed and bound by
Meriden-Stinehour Press.